GEORG BÜCHNER

by Ronald Hauser

Georg Büchner (1813-1837), long recognized by the Germans as one of their most intriguing and brilliant literary figures, has won a certain critical acclaim in America only in recent years. His works fill but a slender volume, but they foreshadow some of the major themes of modern thought and anticipate many of the changes which have transformed the theatre during the last fifty years.

More obviously relevant today than at his own time is his concept of the self-destructive nature of the human intellect. What is usually called "sanity" is taken to be a commonly held system of delusions, and in examining this system, Büchner finds that it is bound to lead to "insane" behavior founded upon myth and baseless conjecture. On the other hand, much of what is labeled by society as "insane" behavior is, in fact, a rational response to a reality which cannot be fathomed. Unlike most other writers, Büchner does not find the flaw in social structures and conventions but rather in the limitations of the human brain. In the comedy *Leonce and Lena* he proposes the madhouse as the ideal solution to the problems of the human condition. The bitter irony of such an ideal is self-evident. In the tragedies *Danton's Death* and *Woyzeck* as well as in the short biographical narrative about the "insane" German poet Lenz, the "sanely insane" protagonists are confronted by a world dominated by seemingly sane forces which are, in truth, totally devoid of rationality.

The present study explores the many facets of this theme and offers an interpretation and stylistic analysis of all of Büchner's works designed especially for the American reader.

TWAYNE'S WORLD AUTHORS SERIES (TWAS)

The purpose of TWAS is to survey the major writers —novelists, dramatists, historians, poets, philosophers, and critics—of the nations of the world. Among the national literatures covered are those of Australia, Canada, China, Eastern Europe, France, Germany, Greece, India, Italy, Japan, Latin America, the Netherlands, New Zealand, Poland, Russia, Scandinavia, Spain, and the African nations, as well as Hebrew, Yiddish, and Latin Classical literatures. This survey is complemented by Twayne's United States Authors Series and English Authors Series.

The intent of each volume in these series is to present a critical-analytical study of the works of the writer; to include biographical and historical material that may be necessary for understanding, appreciation, and critical appraisal of the writer; and to present all material in clear, concise English—but not to vitiate the scholarly content of the work by doing so.

Georg Büchner

By RONALD HAUSER

*State University of New York
at Buffalo*

ABOUT THE AUTHOR

Ronald Hauser, born in Stuttgart, Germany, immigrated to the United States in 1938 at the age of 11. He attended schools in California and received his Ph.D. in German Literature at the University of California (Berkeley) in 1957. He has taught at Northwestern University, Smith College, and the University of Massachusetts (Amherst). Since 1966 he has been at the State University of New York at Buffalo where he served for a time as Associate Provost of Arts and Letters.

Though he now works largely in the area of contemporary German literature, his previous publications include articles on Büchner and other nineteenth-century literary subjects.

Twayne Publishers, Inc.   ::   New York

Library of Congress Cataloging in Publication Data

Hauser, Ronald.
 Georg Büchner.

  (Twayne's world authors series, TWAS 300.   Germany)
  Bibliography: p.
  1.   Büchner, Georg, 1813–1837.
PT1828.B6H3   821'.7   73–17183
ISBN 0–8057–2183–5

To the memory of Hans M. Wolff

Acknowledgments

I would like to express my appreciation to my colleagues Peter Heller and David G. Richards for their advice in the preparation of this study.

The passages quoted from Georg Büchner, *Complete Plays and Prose*, translated and with an introduction by Carl Richard Mueller, copyright 1963 by Carl Richard Mueller, are reprinted with the permission of Hill and Wang, a division of Farrar, Straus & Giroux, Inc.

Contents

Acknowledgments

Chronology

1. Georg Büchner, 1813–1837   13
2. *Danton's Death*—The Quest for Inner Peace   24
3. *Lenz*—The Edge of Insanity   49
4. *Leonce and Lena*—Over the Edge   72
5. *Woyzeck*—The Enemy Within   93
6. The Reception   127
   Notes and References   139
   Selected Bibliography   149
   Index   155

Chronology

1813   Born in Goddelau near Darmstadt, Germany.

1816   Moved to Darmstadt.

1825   Entered Ludwig Georg Gymnasium in Darmstadt.

1831   Began his studies at the University of Strasbourg.

1833   Continued his studies at the University of Giessen.

1834   *"Der Hessische Landbote" (The Hessian Courier)* written in collaboration with Friedrich Ludwig Weidig. Returned to Darmstadt.

1835   *Dantons Tod (Danton's Death)* written in January and February. Fled the country to avoid arrest for political activities. Continued his studies in Strasbourg.

1836   *Sur le système nerveux du barbeau (On the Nervous System of the Barbel)* which earned him membership in the *Société d'histoire naturelle* and then, in September, the Doctor of Philosophy. Translated two Victor Hugo plays into German. Began to compose *Lenz, Leonce und Lena (Leonce and Lena)*, and *Woyzeck*. Gave an inaugural lecture, *"Über Schädelnerven" (On the Cranial Nerves)*, in November at the University of Zurich. Took up a position as Lecturer at the University of Zurich.

1837   Died in Zurich.

CHAPTER 1

Georg Büchner, 1813–1837

NOT until fifty years after his death did Georg Büchner gain a general reputation as one of the great German writers in his native country, and at least another fifty years passed before he gained international recognition. His ever increasing popularity testifies to his kinship with contemporary thought; indeed, at times it seems incredible that Büchner was addressing a world so different from our own, for the problems he poses and the ideas he generates seem so closely associated with this century. That he was all but unknown in the middle decades of the nineteenth century, however, cannot be ascribed to his being out of joint with his time. Actually, he was perfectly in tune with it: a disillusioned revolutionary in a world where one revolutionary movement after another collapsed. Büchner's lack of influence on his contemporaries resulted from his early death and the circumstances which prevented a reasonably complete edition of his works and papers until 1879.[1]

Büchner was only twenty-three years old when he became one of the victims of a minor typhus epidemic in Zurich. Until he recognized the fatal symptoms of his disease, he had every reason to expect that he was destined for great success, not only as a writer, but also as a scientist and academician. Indeed, his whole life seemed pointed toward great accomplishments. He was born on October 17, 1813, the oldest of the six children of Ernst Büchner, a physician, an enlightened liberal, and an admirer of Napoleonic reforms in Germany. The family was financially secure, and there is no evidence of any crisis which might have affected Georg in his childhood. While his father hoped to awaken scientific interests in him, his mother imparted her love of the arts, particularly poetry. When Georg was three years old, the family moved from the small town of Goddelau to nearby Darmstadt, the capital of the Grand Duchy of Hesse. Outside the family home, life was not as serene as it was within. The first years of Büchner's life coincided with the collapse of Napoleonic power. The political turmoil which followed affected particularly the smaller German states, including Hesse, where, throughout Büchner's formative years, an air of increasing oppression prevailed. Undoubtedly encouraged by the generally liberal atmosphere of his home life, Büchner, as a student at Darmstadt's *Gymnasium*, seems to have had a particular fondness for developing ideas which made his teachers feel somewhat uneasy. His eloquent defense of suicide in a school essay on Cato,[2] for example, shows an independence of thought which teachers do not always appreciate. In any case, the final report issued, upon Büchner's graduation, by the director of the *Gymnasium* lauds the student's superior achievement in all subjects except mathematics, but includes the following, only thinly disguised, criticism: "We hold a much too favorable opinion of his clear and penetrating mind ever to imagine that he would stand in the way of his own success through indolence, negligence, or rashly pronounced judgments."[3] These remarks were clearly meant as a warning to the authorities at the University of Strasbourg, to whom they were addressed, that Büchner, though he had a brilliant mind, was a bit of a freethinker.

High-minded, ingenious, full of vitality, reserved in his relationships to others, wide-ranging in literary tastes (with a special love for Shakespeare, Homer, Goethe, Aeschylus and Sophocles), especially talented in the sciences, intensely interested in religious discussions (in which he revealed himself as a skeptic but not as an atheist), politically radical, bitterly critical of all artifice, including such philosophical systems as Hegelian dialectics, contemptuous of those who feed on lifeless formulations instead of devoting themselves to a search for truth, scornful of arbitrary authority, devoted to the ideal of freedom—such are the main strokes of a character sketch attempted by two school friends almost half a century after Büchner left Darmstadt to study medicine at Strasbourg.[4] The image is that of a highly gifted young man who is respected for his integrity and his genuine engagement in the problems of his day, whether scientific, religious, political, or philosophical.

With such wide horizons, it is no wonder that Büchner very quickly became one of the central figures of a large group of serious and active students at Strasbourg, where he matriculated in November, 1831. Only sixteen months after the July revolution this city must have offered a sharp contrast to the oppression in Hesse. Here was a German-speaking city, steeped in German culture, but offering the political freedom of France under Louis Philippe and the Constitutional Charter of 1830. It is hardly surprising that Strasbourg became one of the gathering places of liberals and revolutionaries from those unfortunate little countries across the Rhine where new laws of suppression made life more and more intolerable to anyone possessed by the idea of freedom. The so-called "parliament" of the German Federation, dominated by the Austrian regime of Metternich, even made the mere advocacy of constitutional rights a punishable crime. Extradition of all political "criminals" became binding upon the states of the Federation, but in Strasbourg, on the left bank of the Rhine, scores of German freedom fighters who faced severe penalties for their belief in democratic reform found safety from arrest. Büchner's political radicalism, which had caused concern at Darmstadt, was in perfect harmony with conditions here. Open political discussions, speeches, rallies, and demonstrations were a part of daily student life. There is even reason to suspect his association with one of the most radical revolutionary organizations of the time, the *Société des Droits de l'Homme et du Citoyen*, which had a very active chapter in Strasbourg.[5] But regardless of whether or not he actually became a member, Büchner's political conscience, undoubtedly stimulated by the contrast between Darmstadt and Strasbourg, led him to convictions closely resembling those of the *Société*. In a letter to his family dated April 5, 1833, he explains his attitude toward the German situation:

If there is to be something which can help in our time, it must be force. We know what to expect from our princes. Everything they have granted has been forced from them by necessity. . . . Young people are criticized for their use of violence, but are we not caught in a constant state of violence? Because we are born and raised in a dungeon, we no longer even notice that we are in a pit, with our hands and feet chained to the wall and our mouths gagged. What do you call a lawful state of affairs? A law which makes the great mass of citizens into drudging cattle in order to satisfy the unnatural desires of an insignificant and decadent minority? And this law, maintained by naked military power and by the stupid cleverness of its officials, is the constant exercise of crude force committed against justice and sound reason; and I will fight it with my voice and hand wherever I can.[6]

These words seem to be a declaration of war on the status quo in Germany. Yet Büchner did not pledge himself to limitless warfare. As powerfully as his rage against the tyranny of the ruling class is expressed in this letter, there is a striking measure of restraint in his personal devotion to the cause of violent revolution. While he saw force against the princes as the only hope for Germany, he pointedly avoided dedicating himself to acts of violence and vowed only the use of his "voice and hand"—that is, his spoken and written word—in the fight for freedom. Büchner himself gives the reason for this restraint when he continues in the same letter: "If I have not taken part in those uprisings which have already occurred and do not take part in those which may occur, it is not out of either disapproval or fear, but only because I consider every revolutionary movement useless under present conditions and do not share the delusion of those who see the German nation as a people prepared to fight for its rights." The nineteen-year-old student's enthusiasm for revolution was tempered by his unusually sharp insight into the German problem. The Germans were victimized not only by their rulers but also by their own love for order, which did not allow them, like the French, to rise up in a wave to fight for their rights. Besides containing Büchner's political credo during his second year in Strasbourg, his letter also echoes the deep frustration of a young man who has come to realize that the only possibility for the future of his country—revolution—is, in fact, an impossibility.

Büchner was to spend only two academic years in Strasbourg. In retrospect, he was to consider them his happiest years. Not only did he thrive in the comparatively liberal atmosphere, but he also enjoyed success in his studies and in his personal life. He fell in love and was secretly engaged to Wilhelmine Jaegle, the daughter of a Protestant pastor in whose house he lodged. She was three years his senior, seems to have been completely devoted to him, and, according to the report of one of Büchner's friends, had a calming and moderating influence upon him.[7] But in 1833 Büchner was compelled to transfer to the University at Giessen to conform to a law which forced all Hessian university candidates to spend at least two years at the state's own institution.

How despairing Büchner was once back in his homeland is reflected in his letters of the time, especially those addressed to Wilhelmine: "Since I crossed the Rhine, I feel as if I were inwardly annihilated, not a single emotion stirs within me. I am an automaton; my soul has been taken from me," he wrote shortly after arriving in Giessen.[8] In this tight little city of about 7,000 inhabitants, which looked "horrid" to him from the beginning, everything seemed to conspire to make the twenty-year-old student miserable. After Strasbourg, the routine arrests of students for political reasons must have disgusted him. A desperate loneliness seized him: "My friends are deserting me," he complained;[9] and, indeed, he seems to have lived in almost total isolation. A fellow medical student was later to give the following account in his memoirs:

Frankly we did not find this Georg Büchner sympathetic. He wore a high top hat which always sat at the back of his head. He constantly made a face like a cat during a thunderstorm, kept completely to himself, went around only with a somewhat degenerate and ragged intellectual, August Becker. . . . His reserve was interpreted as arrogance, and since he was obviously involved in political activities, had even dropped revolutionary remarks on one or two occasions, it happened not infrequently that a group of us, coming from a tavern, stopped in front of his house to shout out an ironic acclamation: "Long live Georg Büchner, upholder of the European equilibrium, abolisher of the slave trade!" He acted as if he heard none of the hooting, although his burning lamp showed that he was at home.[10]

Disliked and mocked by his fellow students, unhappy in his studies, in poor health after a relatively light attack of meningitis which, nevertheless, confined him to bed the better part of five weeks, Büchner had abundant cause for his depressions: "My mind is completely unhinged. Work is impossible, a dull brooding has taken hold of me, I am hardly capable of a single lucid thought."[11]

It was during this period of extreme inner anguish, early in 1834, that Büchner became personally engaged in revolutionary action. Short-lived as his actual involvement was, its consequences were to structure the rest of his life. Together with three of his fellow students, August Becker, Gustav Clemm, and Karl Minnigerode, he founded an underground organization, which was named *Society for Human Rights,* undoubtedly after the *Société des Droits de l'Homme.*[12] The structure of this society was distinctly patterned after the French model. Unlike other German student organizations which were connected with the expanding—though illegal—fraternal movements, the Society for Human Rights did not restrict its membership to students, but was meant to appeal especially to the masses. The primary task which the organization set for itself was to prepare the Hessian people, mostly peasants and artisans, for a mass uprising against the oppressive regime of Ludwig II. Besides the original chapter in Giessen, the society had formed a branch at Darmstadt by Easter, 1834.

The group quite obviously planned to wage a propaganda campaign not only against the regime, but also against the social structure of Hesse. Only one manifesto is known to have been printed, *Der Hessische Landbote* (The Hessian Courier), which was written by Büchner in collaboration with Friedrich Ludwig Weidig, a forty-two-year-old veteran of liberal causes. The original text had been composed by Büchner, but Weidig edited it freely, changing Büchner's target from "the rich" to "the aristocrats," and adding several passages containing religious and biblical references.[13] In July, 1834, the clandestine pamphlet was ready. Members of the society were to distribute copies among the peasants in surrounding villages. Hardly had this task begun when Minnigerode was arrested while attempting to enter Giessen with a bundle of pamphlets. The authorities had apparently been informed of the plot.[14]

As soon as Büchner learned of the arrest, he set out to warn other members of the group. Near midnight of the same day (August 1) he reached Weidig's house in the village of Butzbach, where he also found Becker. They decided that Büchner should attempt to alert their comrades in Offenbach, where the pamphlet was printed, before the authorities closed in. He traveled throughout the night and reached Offenbach by noon of the next day. On his way back to Giessen, he thought it wise to make a detour through Frankfurt because he felt that the road was safer from surveillance.

His caution was not exaggerated. When he arrived in Giessen, he found that his room had been searched and his papers confiscated. Having evaded arrest, he was in a good position to confront the authorities in the role of an irate victim of false accusations. He demanded explanations for the illegal search, and since there seems to have been nothing compromising among his papers, he gained enough time to make an unobtrusive exit from the city. Late in August he returned to the parental house in Darmstadt. His career as a leader of a revolutionary movement came to a frustrating end before he reached the age of twenty-one.

Some of the other members of the Society for Human Rights were less fortunate than Büchner. Although the trip to Offenbach had saved at least one member from arrest, Becker, Clemm, and Minnigerode were all sentenced to long prison terms.[15] Weidig, who in November, 1834, attempted to distribute a second, somewhat milder edition of the *Courier*, suffered several arrests and finally was driven to suicide through constant police harassment.

Darmstadt was no permanent haven for Büchner. He knew that it was only a matter of time until the investigation in Giessen and Offenbach would lead to his doorstep. He went so far as to place a ladder against the house to provide a fast emergency exit. His father was totally unaware of Büchner's political involvements and could be expected to react with "the most extreme severity," if they came to light.[16] This fact added to the already overpowering tensions under which Büchner lived, and, since no financial support could be expected from the family, made planning a flight from the country all the more difficult. Büchner's only confidant was his brother Wilhelm, who helped him to plot an escape. In a desperate attempt to provide himself with funds, Büchner decided to write a play based upon the French Revolution. In a few weeks in January and February, 1835, he composed *Dantons Tod* (Danton's Death). On February 21, he sent the manuscript to the publisher Sauerländer in Frankfurt with an urgent plea to forward it to Karl Gutzkow, at that time considered the leading young German literary man of outspoken liberal persuasion.

Gutzkow's actions, as well as his letters of encouragement, attest to the impact *Danton* had on him. Apparently informed of Büchner's dilemma, he wrote: "I can bear to hear anything except that you are going to America. You must stay close by (Switzerland or France), from where you can weave your magnificent gifts into the fabric of German literature."[17] In response to Büchner's immediate need for money, Gutzkow successfully urged Sauerländer to publish *Danton*, although dramas, as he pointed out, were not a lucrative publishing venture. Less than two weeks after the manuscript had been submitted, a sum, albeit a small one, was made available by Sauerländer and forwarded to Darmstadt by Gutzkow, who even offered to deliver it in person.[18] It arrived too late to reach him. Only through the ruse of sending his brother in his place had Büchner been able to avoid appearing at an investigative hearing into his activities. He knew that arrest was at hand. By March 9, he had crossed the border into France. To his family he wrote that he would devote all his efforts to his studies in the "medical-philosophical sciences, a field in which there is still enough room to accomplish something worthwhile." As he had felt the weight of oppression descending upon him when he crossed the Rhine into Germany a year and a half earlier, so he now felt elation and the easing of the all but unbearable tensions: "Since I have crossed the border, I have a renewed spirit of life; I stand completely alone now, but precisely that intensifies my powers."[19]

Büchner's second visit to Strasbourg was an almost unbelievably productive one. Within the period of eighteen months he completed his studies, produced a dissertation on the nervous system of the barbel in French (for which he was awarded the doctorate in September, 1836), and delivered three papers to the Strasbourg Society of Natural History, which honored him with a membership and the publication of his dissertation. To earn money, he translated two Victor Hugo dramas, *Lucrèce Borgia* and *Marie Tudor*, for Sauerländer, despite his artistic disdain for them.

All the rest of his literary works also fall into this period. The drama *Leonce and Lena*, written as an entry in a comedy competition sponsored by the publishing house of Cotta, and the novella *Lenz*, apparently intended for one of Gutzkow's periodicals, were composed in the spring of 1836. During the summer of the same year, Büchner worked on two dramas, *Woyzeck* and presumably *Pietro Aretino*.[20] The former has been preserved only in an incomplete, hardly legible manuscript, while *Pietro Aretino* has been lost altogether. There is every indication that both works were completed or at least very close to completion by January, 1837.[21]

Büchner's dissertation, "On the Nervous System of the Barbel," was so highly regarded that he had no difficulty in arranging for a trial lecture at the University of Zurich in the hope of receiving an appointment as lecturer. Delivered in November, 1836, this lecture, "On the Cranial Nerves," shows the continuity of Büchner's specialized scientific interest in the nature of the nervous system, and, at the same time, reflects his desire to steer a course in the direction of philosophy.[22] Besides offering a comparative anatomy of the cranial nerves, it contains fundamental speculations on the nature of existence. The lecture led to the desired result. In the winter semester of 1836–37, Büchner, not certain until the last moment whether he wanted to offer a course in philosophy or zoology, began a series of lectures on the "Comparative Anatomy of Fishes and Amphibians."[23]

The crossing of the border into Switzerland in October, 1836, was cause for some anxiety. Swiss authorities, due to pressure from the German states, were hesitant about allowing political refugees to enter. Büchner's appearance in Zurich was made possible only with the help of certification from Strasbourg police authorities that he had engaged in no political activities since leaving his native country.[24] Indeed, there is every indication that Büchner carefully avoided close contact with revolutionary cliques among the refugees in both Strasbourg and Zurich. The political statements in his letters of this period have a tone of both hopelessness and disengagement. The most outspoken one, addressed to Gutzkow, ends in utter disenchantment: "For what purpose should such a thing as this [decadent modern society] walk around between heaven and earth? Its entire life consists only of attempts to rid itself of the most horrible boredom. Let it die out; that is the only new thing which it can still experience."[25]

In Zurich, Büchner led a rather quiet life. He moved within a small circle of friends, mostly fellow refugees, who were colleagues at the university. Closest to him were Wilhelm Friedrich Schulz and his wife Caroline, who had followed the same trail from Darmstadt to Strasbourg and had arrived in Zurich only a month before Büchner. He frequently took walks with them, but on February 2 he did not feel well enough to join them. On the evening of the same day, Caroline, who reported the daily progress of Büchner's illness in her diary, urged him to go to bed.[26] During the following days, his condition gradually worsened. On February 10, he attempted to get up in order to write, but was too weak. Not until the 15th was the seriousness of the illness recognized. By this time, delirium had begun, interrupted only rarely by moments of lucidity. Caroline arranged to have one of his friends constantly at his bedside. On the 16th, his weak pulse and rapid heartbeat led the doctors to give up all hope. Caroline, in desperation, aimed the question, "Why?," at the heavens. To calm her, her husband reportedly said: "Our friend himself gives you the answer. Just a moment ago, after a powerful storm of fantasies had passed, he spoke in a quiet, elevated, solemn voice the words: 'We do not suffer too much pain, we suffer too little, for only through pain do we enter into God! We are death, dust, and ashes, how dare we lament?' "[27] Whether or not Büchner actually spoke these words is uncertain, but they constitute the last lucid thoughts that can be attributed to him. The next day, he was barely able to recognize his fiancée, who had been summoned from Strasbourg by Caroline. On February 19, 1837, ("it was Sunday, the sky was blue, and the sun was shining,") Büchner died in the presence of his beloved Wilhelmine.[28]

Of his literary work only *Danton's Death* had reached a limited public at the time of his death. In the obituary, written by Wilhelm Schulz for the *Züricher Zeitung*, there is an announcement that the as yet unpublished works would soon be in print.[29] This prediction was only partially fulfilled. Gutzkow, who wanted to prepare a collected edition of the works and papers—the only way of making the name of Büchner known to his own generation—failed to get the cooperation of the Büchner family. Nevertheless, he arranged for the publication of excerpts from *Leonce and Lena* (1838) and *Lenz* (1839). The papers and manuscripts were scattered. Some were in possession of Büchner's friends in Zurich. Besides a great many letters, Wilhelmine held some manuscripts, probably including Büchner's diary.[30] The family in Darmstadt, of course, was in the possession of the bulk of the material.

The Büchner family did make some efforts to have a collected edition published, but nothing came of it until 1850, when Büchner's younger brother, Ludwig, edited a collection containing *Leonce and Lena, Lenz,* and a selected group of letters. Not long afterwards, a fire at the Büchner house destroyed many of the papers.

What the world knows of Georg Büchner it owes primarily to the painstaking work of Karl Emil Franzos in the 1870's. Sparing no effort, he not only collected manuscripts, letters, and other documents pertaining to Büchner's life, but sought out, interviewed, and corresponded with as many people who had known Büchner personally as he could find. His labors produced the critical edition of 1879, which, despite some glaring deficiencies, formed the basis for all subsequent editions.

Unfortunately, Wilhelmine, who never married, refused access to her treasured mementos. When she died in 1880, not a single document of Büchner's could be found among her effects. Presumably she had destroyed everything. Besides the drama *Pietro Aretino*, and the final manuscript of *Woyzeck*, an undetermined number of letters and, perhaps most unfortunately, Büchner's diary, which, according to Caroline Schulz, contained "rich intellectual treasures," were thus lost.[31]

CHAPTER 2

Danton's Death

The Quest for Inner Peace

THE fact that *Danton's Death* was written under the fear of arrest for revolutionary activities has led early interpreters to see in it a drama intended to promote political and social revolution.[1] *The Hessian Courier*, after all, spells out a clear and unmistakable message. "Freedom for the huts! War on the palaces!" is its motto, and the opening sentence indicates its uncompromising tone: "The life of the aristocrats is a long Sunday: they live in beautiful houses, they wear elegant clothes, they have fat faces, and they speak a language of their own; whereas the people lie at their feet like manure on the fields."[2] After seeing his revolutionary ambitions stifled through the arrest of his comrades and the confiscation of the *Courier*, it seems only logical that Büchner should pursue the theme of revolution in his first literary work. The French Revolution was the great inspiration for the German revolutionary spirits of the nineteenth century. However, given Büchner's political convictions, as documented in the *Courier*, it seems surprising that he did not focus upon the uprising of the French people and the overthrow of the aristocracy, but rather upon the Reign of Terror which followed. Specifically, he portrays those black days of the revolution when the revolutionary movement sent its own heroes to the guillotine. If he had really wanted to advance the cause of revolution in Germany with *Danton*, he could hardly have chosen a more self-defeating vehicle. This fact alone casts grave doubts on the view that *Danton* was inspired by the same passions which engendered the *Courier*.

Much more valid is the more recently explored view that *Danton* is an expression of Büchner's deep frustration which followed the collapse of the "Society for Human Rights," a frustration brought on not only through the swift action of the authorities, but also by the inability of the conspirators to agree on either revolutionary goals or methods. In interpretations based on this conception, the drama emerges as a total disavowal of all possible political solutions to the problems of mankind.[3]

Most hostile to this line of interpretation are those critics who see in *Danton* an affirmation of Marxist dogma. To them, *Danton* represents the tragedy of a man who, despite his position of power, has lost his belief in the principles of the revolution and must be destroyed along with his followers to safeguard those principles.[4] While such interpretations can point to a semblance of unity in political tendency between the *Courier* and *Danton,* they face the all but impossible task of arousing sympathy for Danton's opponents, the chilling dogmatists Robespierre and Saint-Just. To be sure, an audience of convinced Marxists should be able to dispense with sympathy in favor of political realism, but Büchner could hardly have hoped for such an audience in the Germany of 1835. It would not have been difficult for him to show Robespierre's actions as at least indirectly responsive to the people's cry for bread, but he chose, instead, to portray Robespierre as responsive only to the people's thirst for blood.

Political interpretations of *Danton* have been less than totally convincing. For this reason, and under the influence of the new directions in criticism, the more recent interpretations have tended to ignore the discrepancies between the political views of the author and those expressed in his work and have concentrated on close examination and analysis of the text.[5] The great advantage of such textual explications when applied to *Danton* is their emphasis on form and structure, for it is the use of language, the imagery, the symbolism, the juxtaposition of terms, the use of the short fragmented scene that make Büchner's drama unique and give it the impact which has carried it to ever increasing prominence.[6]

The relative lack of importance given to the plot is shown by the fact that the title, *Danton's Death,* in itself reduces dramatic tension. To all those who are even vaguely familiar with the events of the French Revolution of 1789, Büchner's title conjures up an image of that great orator and spiritual leader of the Revolution, who made only feeble efforts to save himself and his close followers when he came under attack by Robespierre and the Jacobins. In contrast to the radical Girondins who had used the guillotine as a platform for fiery speeches before they died, Danton and his adherents followed them to the guillotine in stark silence.

Büchner takes over the historical image of Danton without essential change; indeed, his dialogue sometimes consists of verbatim quotations from the public records which he found in his source materials.[7] He follows the historical accounts so closely that his first publisher, apparently noting the play's lack of traditional dramatic structure, felt obliged to add the cautious subtitle "Dramatic Scenes from the French Reign of Terror."[8] Undoubtedly because this subtitle shows a total lack of understanding for his dramatic intentions, Büchner indicated in a letter that he was offended by it. In the same letter, he attempted to describe these intentions in the following terms: "In my eyes, the dramatic poet is nothing but a writer of history, but he stands above the latter inasmuch as he creates history for the second time and, instead of giving us a dry narrative, places us directly into the life of an epoch. Instead of characteristics, he gives us characters, instead of descriptions, living figures."[9] Büchner's dramatic interest does not lie in the events of the Reign of Terror from which he derives his plot, but rather in the spirit which governed these events. It is not important what happens to Danton; what is important is Danton as a man whose life is not synonymous with political convictions and public appearances.

Precisely by using the already existing historical image of Danton in those scenes which show him as a public figure, Büchner throws special light upon those which reflect his inner life. The structure of the drama is akin to a collage in which clippings and fragments are pasted over a photographically realistic sketch of a well-known scene. The background image is allowed to show through here and there, enough to be readily recognizable, but the artistic effect of the whole work is achieved through the brilliant juxtaposition of the superimposed materials.

The first scene of *Danton* is composed of a number of such carefully juxtaposed scraps. The stage directions indicate the theme: Danton's friend, Hérault de Séchelles, is seen playing cards with a group of women, while Danton is sitting at some distance from the others on a footstool at the feet of his wife, Julie. The tableau is immediately recognizable as a social gathering, but Danton is not engaged in the evening's activity; isolated from the group, he converses privately with his wife. The structure of the scene allows the dialogue to move back and forth between the two focal points, the card players on the one hand, and the two isolated guests on the other. While Danton is in a position to observe the gathering at the cardtable, the players, immersed in their game, are oblivious to him. Two completely independent conversations are interlaced, seemingly at random. But even before a single word is spoken, Danton's voluntary alienation becomes a visual reality. Even among his friends, he is seen as an outsider, a lonely spectator of life.

This first visual impression is immediately reinforced by Danton's opening words. With a glance in the direction of the cardtable, he says: "Look at that lovely lady! She knows how to play her cards right. They say she gives her *coeur* to her husband and her *carreau* to everybody else. You women could make a man fall in love with a lie."[10] While the opening sentences set an earthy tone right from the beginning of the drama, they appear to be nothing more than idle gossip. Using card symbolism, Danton tells his wife the latest rumors concerning one of the women at the cardtable. Since this woman is not specifically identified, no real importance attaches itself to the words themselves. However, the last sentence of the passage shows that Danton is not just gossiping, but is actually attempting to give expression to his lack of rapport, not only with the players, but also with Julie herself. While the literal meaning of the sentence is somewhat vague, its message is evident. To fall in love with a lie shows a desire to be deceived. However, since one cannot be deceived unless one is unaware of the deception, Danton's words also contain the plea of the intellect for a haven from awareness.

That the desire for illusion precludes any human relationship based on trust escapes Julie, for she responds with the question, "Do you believe in me?," and Danton's answer leaves no more doubt about the completeness of his isolation: "What do I know? We know very little about one another. We are thick-skinned; we reach out our hands toward one another, but our efforts are in vain, we are just rubbing leather against leather—we are very lonely." Even the most intimate relationship, that between man and wife, is but illusion for Danton. Büchner's taut prose allows him instantly to demonstrate the correlation between Danton's words and the immediate reality. Julie's previous response had already shown less than a complete understanding of Danton's thoughts; now she reveals her "thick-skinned" nature even more clearly. Even while the lack of understanding between people is the topic of conversation, its relevance to the immediate situation is demonstrated through Julie's own lack of understanding. Apparenty considering Danton's "we" a purely philosophical abstraction referring to mankind in general, she says, "You know me, Danton."

Danton is talking at Julie, not to her, but her simple responses do allow him to expand his theme: "Yes, knowing is what it's called. You have dark eyes and curly hair and a nice complexion, and you always say 'dear Georges' to me! But [*he touches her forehead and eyes*] there, what is lurking in there? Go on, we have coarse senses. Know one another? We would have to crack open our skulls and tear the thoughts out of each other's brain fibers." To frame this segment of the discussion, Büchner, at this point, shifts momentarily to the conversation at the cardtable. The abrupt shift, along with the shock effect of Danton's concluding image, serves to drive the message home. Anticipating the methods applied by the dramatists of Expressionism the better part of a century later, Büchner hews Danton's character out of the rough stone of history with a few bold strokes. In contrast to traditional dramatic techniques, where character is gradually revealed through personal interaction and introspection, Danton asserts his personality in a few vigorous formulations, the meaning of which is communicated to the audience but not to those at whom they are directed.

The basis of Danton's alienation is his awareness that "we" cannot know anything, least of all other human beings. As the last sentence in the statement above indicates, this human fault does not lie in the brain, which is a sensitive organ capable of producing thought, but in the senses, which are too "coarse" to communicate adequate information to allow the brain to distinguish between reality and illusion. This fault, according to Danton, is shared by all men. What distinguishes him from most others is his realization of this condition. Once the inability to distinguish between reality and illusion is accepted as a concept, both categories cease to exist. The disappearance of these categories leaves open only two possibilities. Either a man makes arbitrary distinctions and acts the role of a fool, not unlike the deluded husband of the woman mentioned in the first lines of the drama, or he refuses to make arbitrary distinctions and is thereby rendered inactive.

This is Danton's condition. His unwillingness to make arbitrary distinctions leads him to a nihilism which cuts so deep that even the question of life and death leaves him indifferent, as his very next words indicate:

DANTON: No, Julie, I love you like the grave.
JULIE: [*turning away from him*] Oh!
DANTON: No, listen to me! People say there is peace in the grave, that the grave and peace are one and the same. If that is so, then I rest beneath the earth whenever I am lying between your thighs. You sweet grave; your lips are the mourning bells, your voice their ring, your breasts my burial mound, and your heart my coffin.

To Danton the greatest possible happiness is absolute peace, the peace found perchance in the grave, but in life only "between maids' legs" to quote Hamlet, whose torment this theme recalls.[11] Like Hamlet, Danton seeks that state of dreamless repose when the mind ceases to function; but, unlike Hamlet, whose despair is rooted in his conception of reality, Danton's suffering seems to be the self-generated product of the mind. The fact that Danton's longing for death is expressed in the very first scene of the drama, before even a hint of an externally induced conflict is presented, strongly indicates that it grows out of pure contemplation on the human condition and is not specifically related to the political struggle portrayed in the drama.

Büchner once more places special emphasis on Danton's words by cutting off the conversation and re-focusing on the carefree action at the cardtable. Referring to the game, one of the players shouts, "Lost!" From its timing within the scene, this exclamation can be construed as being prophetic, for it is abundantly clear that Danton has already lost his game, even though some cards remain to be played.

Only now, after the self-destructive nature of Danton's reflections has been revealed, does Büchner turn to the political conflict. The transition is accomplished through Hérault's series of risqué witticisms playing on the "indecent" relationship between kings, queens, and knaves (jacks) in the deck of cards. While his puns have the tone of moral mockery, the final image has distinct political overtones: "I wouldn't allow my daughter to play this kind of game; it's indecent how the kings and queens fall on top of each other and right afterwards the knaves pop out." Though this pun is put in the mouth of a Dantonist, its irony cuts in all directions. At least two separate visions are masterfully merged into one symbolic image. The morally depraved activities of the aristocrats immediately spawn knaves, that is, imitators from a lower class. By this, Hérault undoubtedly means to symbolize his bitter disappointment over the fact that the aristocrats have so quickly been replaced by new oppressors. However, seen from the point of view of Robespierre and Saint-Just, whose charge against the Dantonists includes, besides moderationism, the accusation of moral decadence, Hérault's pun would have a completely different meaning, a meaning contained in Robespierre's own words from his speech at the Jacobin Club: "You will understand me more easily if you think of those who used to live in attics and now ride in fancy carriages and fornicate with former marquises and baronesses."[12] From this point of view, the knaves are the Dantonists who are endangering the progress of the revolution by adopting the old aristocratic vices. Though Hérault could hardly have intended such an interpretation, it is nevertheless reinforced by the fact that, even while he is speaking, he is seen carousing at the cardtable with "ladies" whose repute has already been placed in question by Danton himself.

Particularly because it introduces the political theme for the first time in the drama, the irony in Hérault's words is a strong indication of Büchner's hate of the depraved aristocrats whose former reign finds no defenders whatever within the work. On the other hand, has either side fully cast out the spirit of the old regime? Are not the two primary evils of aristocratic rule, gluttony and terrorism—both of which Büchner had singled out for attack in the *Courier*—still alive? Have the kings and queens not simply been replaced by knaves? These are the questions which dominate the political conflict of *Danton*, and they lead to a final, all-important question: does a revolution which fails to set aside both evils meet the needs of the people in whose name it is carried out?

The action of the drama would seem to indicate a negative answer to this essential question. The Dantonist's side is presented first. Hérault's card game is interrupted by the arrival of

Danton's Death

Camille Desmoulins and Philippeau, who bring the latest news from the guillotine which, on that same day, had claimed another twenty lives. The executions are cutting ever deeper into the ranks of former revolutionary heroes. The Hébertists have fallen because their revolutionary fervor had engendered even more fear in the people than that of the Decemvirs. Hérault expresses his views of the ruling spirit in these terms: "They would like to make Antediluvians out of us. Saint-Just wouldn't mind if we crawled around on all fours again so that the Advocate from Arras [Robespierre] could invent caps, school benches, and an Almighty God for us according to the mechanics of the watchmaker from Geneva [Rousseau]." Just as the aristocrats reduce man to the level of animals according to Büchner's *Courier,* so does the Committee of Public Safety. Just as the aristocrats hankered for childlike obedience on the part of the people, so do Saint-Just and Robespierre. The oppression and fear of former times are also the spirit of the new era. Even though the new rulers might be guided by the idealistic philosophy of Rousseau rather than by Machiavellian principles, the people's yoke is as tight as ever. The new masters even want to invent a new image of God to replace the one tailored to the specifications of the old order.

How long must the oppression and terror go on? The Dantonists' response is that it must stop now:

PHILIPPEAU: How much longer must we be filthy and bloody like newborn children, have coffins for cradles, and play around with heads? We must move forward: the Committee for Clemency must be instituted, the deposed deputies must be reinstated.
HÉRAULT: The Revolution has reached the stage for reorganization. The Revolution must end, and the Republic must begin.

There can be no doubt that the ideas expressed in these words evoke the author's full sympathy. Philippeau and Hérault raise the cry for freedom—a cry echoed in the hearts of all who know oppression. According to them, the time has come for the people to receive the reward of their struggle. "The Republic must begin," and Hérault goes on to spell out those rewards:

In our laws, rights must be put above obligation, welfare above virtue and protection above punishment. Every man must be able to assert himself and act in accord with his own nature. Whether he is reasonable or unreasonable, educated or simple, good or evil, all that is of no concern to the state. We are all fools, and no one has the right to force his own particular brand of foolishness on others. Everyone must be able to pursue his pleasure in his own way with the exception that no one is permitted to pursue pleasure at the expense of others or to disturb another in his own particular form of enjoyment.

Hérault's words clearly carry the ring of American revolutionary idealism as expressed in the Declaration of Independence. The stress is put upon individualism and particularly upon the "pursuit of happiness." The state is to provide equal protection to all citizens, regardless of the direction of their pursuits, as long as they do not interfere with the rights of others.

As a representation of human ideals, Hérault's conception of the Republic can find little opposition from those who honor freedom. Notably lacking, however, is any consideration for the material needs of the people in their quest for happiness. Hérault's conception is as un-Marxian as it is pre-Marxian. He seems to have no awareness of the limitations imposed upon the freedom of many by the radically unequal distribution of wealth. The exposition of this flaw in Hérault's political program does not come until the second scene. As the first scene draws to a close, the Dantonists represent the voice of liberalism in a world dominated by cross-currents of dogmatism. Robespierre's men are characterized by their opponents as the forces of darkness and oppression, whose only concern is the subjugation of Frenchmen to completely arbitrary principles. By contrast, Danton's friends, with their insistence on freedom of thought, appear as the forces of hope.

Yet Danton himself does not share the hopes of his followers. Indeed, the contrast between Danton's own outlook and the convictions of his followers is as great as that between the two political factions. The dimensions of this contrast within the Dantonist camp, however, lie totally outside the realm of politics. What Hérault considers a problem responsive to political solution, Danton sees in existential proportions. Danton's nihilism, based upon the idea that men can know nothing and no one, finds its counterpart in Hérault's statement: "we are all fools and no one has the right to force his particular brand of foolishness on others." In fact, the essence of Danton's *Weltanschauung* is the intensification of this tenet to its most radical, extrapolitical extreme. Danton understands that the institution of the notion that no man has the right to impose his values on others would, in itself, be an imposition of an ethical value—namely that all values are vain. As much as this particular value might be in tune with his own conceptions, it is still self-annihilating, and political paralysis is its rational consequence. No wonder that Danton refuses to take the cause of his followers onto the floor of the Convention! With a consistency of thought, which nevertheless vexes his politically involved friends, he refuses to champion one foolishness against another.

Why did Danton start to fight in the first place? This is precisely the question Camille puts to him when he realizes that Danton can no longer be relied upon to lead the fight he himself had instigated. Danton's reply is not without irony: "These people [i.e., Robespierre *et al.*] disgusted me. I could never stand to watch such paragons of virtue spread their asses out without giving them a kick. It's just my nature coming through." A close reading of this highly sarcastic retort yields another example of the double meaning so typical of Büchner's concentrated style. On the one hand, it is a destructive parody of Hérault's political ideal: "Every man must be able to assert himself and act in accord with his own nature." In very simple terms, Danton demonstrates the fundamental irony inherent in such doctrines. Since men's "natures" are in conflict with one another, the idea of freedom defined in such terms becomes all but meaningless, for it invites precisely the kind of chaos symbolized by the Reign of Terror. Heavy emphasis is thereby laid upon the necessary limitations—no one is allowed to interfere with another man's natural pursuits, to paraphrase Hérault. In effect, this means that only those "natures" are allowed to assert themselves which are in accord with all others— a meaningless formulation which is as applicable to the most oppressive tyranny as it is to the most liberally constituted democracy.

Besides underscoring the intrinsic futility of even the most liberal conception of freedom, Danton's reply also gives another dimension to his characterization as a nihilist. Actually his words strikingly remind one of the Storm and Stress heroes in the tradition of Goethe's *Götz von Berlichingen*. In Götz and the many dramatic figures patterned after him, spontaneity of action became the highest human ideal as against speculative reasoning which, at best, could lead to error if not to catastrophe. This programmatic inversion of the values of the Enlightenment finds a clear parallel not only in Danton's words—"it's just my nature coming through"—but also in his situation. All those with whom he deals, not even his closest friends excepted, endlessly indulge in more or less dogmatic theories. Danton's scorn for such speculation is brusquely expressed in his last statement of the scene:

[*To Julie*] I have to leave. These people with their politics get on my nerves. [*From the doorway*] Let me make a quick prophecy: The statue of liberty has not yet been cast. The oven glows; we could all burn our fingers on it.

Not only do political discussions irritate him, but, as his "prophecy" indicates, he feels that they lead to nothing. With all their conjectures, Danton's friends have not even cast a tenable definition of liberty.[13] Despite Danton's warning, the end of the scene shows his followers prepared to risk their lives fighting for "freedom," an idea which, though rationally formulated, defies reason.

Danton's explanation that his involvement in the fight against Robespierre and the Committee of Public Safety had been a purely spontaneous reaction to their moral stance, however, falls far short of being a positive assertion of Storm and Stress principles. Even though his relations to the outside world are reminiscent of figures like Götz, he can hardly be considered a martyr for the cause of allowing "nature" to come through. There is not the slightest hint that instinctive action leads to superior results. On the contrary, Danton's implied disavowal of his followers' cause—a cause that had been the spontaneous product of his own nature—also represents a distrust of his inner voice and shows that he has no hope of lightening his existential burdens by allowing free rein to his natural impulses.

Within the first scene, Büchner removes from Danton's character all bases for meaningful action. Danton's distrust, not only of the outside world with its conflicting ideologies, but also of his own "coarse senses" and his inner "nature," is programmatically unveiled. A careful reading of the scene leaves no doubt that the issues are much more fundamental than the political theories incorporated in the drama. In fact, the primary purpose of the political conflict is to emphasize the contrast between nihilism and all forms of dogmatism. Danton's concern is whether the intrinsic human condition is tolerable, regardless of externally imposed social or political systems. Small wonder that attempts to fix Büchner's political sympathies within the drama have not been altogether convincing. The evaluation of political problems was hardly his intention. Indeed, the confusion created by the juxtaposition of two divergent dogmas, neither of which finds total favor or disfavor, would have been a perfect vehicle should the author have wanted to demonstrate the impotence of political solutions in general. As already indicated, the fact that the substance of the political conflict is taken directly from historical sources offers strong support that this was precisely his intention. Büchner simply allows the political sympathies attached to the historical figures and events to remain intact.

Danton's men, moved by the Epicurean ideals of freedom they express in the first scene, come into direct conflict with Robespierre's idea of republicanism which Büchner attempts to present with the objectivity of a historian. As if to offset the clear advantages enjoyed by the Dantonists whose cause is presented first, Büchner immediately introduces a street scene which casts doubts upon the practicality of their ideals of freedom.[14] In grotesque terms, the tragic condition of a man and his wife forced by economic necessity to sell their daughter to a rich man as a prostitute shows that freedom under the doctrine of the "pursuit of pleasure" is heavily dependent upon economic resources. Without sweeping economic reform, the Dantonists' political theories are nothing but a utopian dream. Büchner carefully neutralizes them as possible solutions to the pressing needs of the people even before Robespierre's views are presented.

Central to Robespierre's political philosophy is his belief in a restrictive moral code. According to his conception, without universally accepted moral standards, the Republic is in constant danger of chaotic disintegration. The subjugation of the poor, as revealed in the street scene and the resultant rampage of the mob aimed against everyone rich enough to possess a handkerchief or cultured enough to know how to read and write, certainly does not discredit this idea. In fact, the street scene serves to place

Robespierre's public pronouncements, presented in the very next scene, in the best possible light. A portion of his speech follows:

. . . The arm of the Republic is Terror; the strength of the Republic is Virtue—Virtue because without it Terror is pernicious; Terror because without it Virtue is powerless. Terror is the consequence of Virtue, it is nothing other than swift, stern, and unswerving justice. They say that Terror is the weapon of despotism, and therefore our government is a despotism. Yes! But only insofar as the swords in the hands of heroes who fight for Freedom are like unto sabers with which the satellites of tyrants are armed. . . . The government of this Revolution is the despotism of Freedom against tyranny.[15]

While Hérault's conception of freedom is an expression of impractical idealism, Robespierre's is a rather empty rhetorical formulation. That Robespierre is well aware of the vulnerability of his political theories becomes clear when he feels impelled to define the difference between tyranny and his idea of the Republic. That the line he draws between the two is nothing but an arbitrarily contrived formula is self-evident. He simply labels the Republican troops "the heroes who fight for Freedom."

Büchner's intentions in respect to Robespierre are made abundantly clear from the beginning. He first shows the pressing need for moral reform in the street scene and then focuses upon the moral reformer, who, despite the fact that the people look upon him as the "Messiah,"[16] by his own words condemns himself as a tyrant and makes a mockery of the idea of freedom. If, on the one hand, moral restraint is a prerequisite for freedom, and, on the other, the strict enforcement of moral codes mocks the very idea of freedom, what is freedom but an abstraction with no visible link to the human condition?

With the figure of Robespierre, Büchner demonstrates at once the impossibility of the revolutionary goals and the incredibly cruel irony prevailing in practical political doctrines. Within the framework of the drama, no workable alternative to the Reign of Terror is offered. While the Dantonists, in their demand to stop the killings, are guided by more humanitarian principles, the impractical basis of their program is made clear not only in the first street scene but in all the subsequent folk scenes. To prevent chaotic looting and murdering in the street, the people must be restrained by powerful means. The urgency of this need is decisively demonstrated:

ALL: Kill! Kill!
ROBESPIERRE: In the name of the law!
FIRST CITIZEN: What is the law?
ROBESPIERRE: The will of the people.
FIRST CITIZEN: We are the people and we don't want law; ergo: our will is the law; ergo: in the name of the law there is no more law; ergo: kill![17]

Robespierre's program of terror and virtue responds to the clear and urgent need to keep the Republic from disintegrating into chaos. The ironic fact that in saving the Republic he must destroy its fundamental principle—the law is the will of the people—which he himself mouths here, aptly demonstrates the tragic absurdity of "practical" politics, which, as Büchner sees it, must by necessity lead to some form of tyranny.

There is no question but that Robespierre is "right" in a purely political sense, for he has social necessity on his side. Though the drama gives little direct insight into his character, there is sufficient evidence to conclude that he is not motivated by the pure lust for power. The initial impression that he keeps the guillotine busy in an effort to reduce the murders in the street is never challenged. Yet it is shockingly clear that a world which is forced to place its hopes in the hands of such men, a world which cannot function except under the yoke of terror, is a world without hope.

In a world without hope of a dignified existence free from fear, free from want, and free from the arbitrary rule of oppressors, Danton's lonely position is "right" in a universal sense, for it is the position of hopelessness, the only one which does not compromise truth. It is the only position which does not compromise its own ideals, for it has none, and it is the only position which comprehends the paradoxes of human nature.

The examination of this position is the principal theme of the drama. As the nominal leaders of a political faction calling for individual freedom, Danton and his men constitute a danger to a state which demands total conformity. That their views should lead them to the guillotine is a foregone conclusion conditioned not only by historical fact but also by the needs of the Republic as they are represented in the drama. While the downfall of these men, whose doctrines, no matter how unrealistic, nevertheless capture the sympathy of the audience, is, in itself, a tragedy, the real tragic substance of *Danton's Death* is the gradual revelation that Danton's agonizing *Weltanschauung* is the only view relevant to the world in which he lives.

Büchner's Danton is not a hero with a tragic flaw that makes him incapable of responding successfully to the demands that are made upon him, nor is he an anti-hero whose weakness as a man leads him, as well as those closest to him, to disaster. Danton is a hero in the dramatic tradition of Goethe's *Faust*. No less than Faust, Danton is intended to symbolize modern man. It is no accident that Danton's characterization starts with the same nihilistic concept which forms the basis of Faust's opening monologue. All his struggles have led him to one single realization: he knows that we can know nothing.

If Faust is saved from the suicidal desperation to which this realization leads, it is not because he represents a fundamentally different spirit, but because he lives in a fundamentally different world. Danton's world is stripped of the cosmic superstructure which is the prime mover in Faust's world. While Goethe presupposes the existence of supernatural forces in *Faust*, Büchner makes the opposite assumption. Danton faces a world in which man must depend exclusively upon his own resources.

This difference in world perspective makes a closer comparison of the two dramatic works unrewarding despite certain incontrovertible similarities. Danton is anything but an imitation of Faust, but Büchner's drama is a tragedy in the same sense that *Faust* is a tragedy despite the "happy ending" of the second part. Both the Renaissance scholar and the eighteenth-century revolutionary symbolize man as a tragically inadequate creature who falters before an existence grown spiritually precarious, undermined by the erosive force of questions the answers to which elude him. That Danton's skepticism should lead him to an uninhibited Epicureanism not unlike Faust's does not represent a literary debt but is the natural outgrowth of his mental state. If all other criteria for orienting oneself are lacking in a world which cannot be grasped intellectually, then the "coarse senses," as Danton calls them, are the only reality and their titillation the only substance of life.

Epicureanism is the one bond which ties Danton to his followers. However, as has been shown already, for them the "pursuit of pleasure" is not dictated by existential desperation but offers a positive political alternative. While Danton shares their dream, he does not share their hopes. Camille, who throughout the drama is closest to Danton and might even be considered his alter ego—Danton himself calls him his "echo"—expresses this dream in the following terms:[18] ". . . We want naked gods, bacchic priestesses, Olympian revelries, and from melodic lips: wicked love which brings tranquillity to our limbs. . . . Our divine Epicurus and Venus with her beautiful buttocks must become the doorkeepers of the Republic in place of the sacred Marat and Chalier."[19] Camille's dream of the future of the Republic represents an image of a world in which Danton's life might find dignified expression. But turning France into a paradisiacal Greece is no more possible in the modern world than a Faustlike journey into the classical past in the absence of supernatural intervention. Danton is condemned to search for pleasure in the streets of Paris. At a crucial moment in the drama when his followers first realize the precariousness of their position they know where to look for Danton:

LEGENDRE: Where is Danton?
LACROIX: How should I know? He's looking for the Venus de'Medici piecemeal among all the whores of the Palais Royal; he's making a mosaic, as he puts it. God only knows what limb he is working on now. Pity that nature cuts up beauty in such small pieces, like Medea her brothers, and deposits them haphazardly in people's bodies.[20]

The Palais Royal turned into a brothel is the closest approximation to the "Olympian revelries" which the real world has to offer. Here only great ingenuity can create an illusion of "Venus." Yet Danton throws himself completely into the task. Even while his fate is being sealed at the Jacobin Club, he is captivated by a girl whose name happens to be Marion—though Rosalie has the beautiful hips, and Adelaide has a face so striking that one does not notice her body: "Why can't I contain every part of your beauty inside me, hold it in my arms? . . . I wish I were a part of air that I could bathe you all about in my flood, break myself on every cape of your body."[21] As they are spoken, these words, which have a clearly poetic ring (at least in German), appear to be the expression of Danton's genuine feelings. This is the only moment in the drama when he seems to show any enthusiasm whatever for life. But this image, no sooner created, is immediately shattered when Lacroix enters with Rosalie and Adelaide, and it becomes obvious that Danton's relationship to Marion is no more than the ordinary relationship with a prostitute. The sham and deception of the bordello, a poor substitute for the "naked gods and bacchic priestesses," reveal themselves in their true light.

The abrupt destruction of the romantic image punctuates the desperation in Danton's situation. On the one hand, it shows that self-deception is the only possibility left to him, while at the same time it reveals the impossibility of sustaining such self-deception. Even though Danton can achieve a momentary state of intoxication, the rudely sobering intrusion of reality makes the tragic irony of his life unmistakably clear: only escape from the realities of life could lead to a state of satisfaction; but the escape is impossible because his mind is incapable of sustaining illusion—it refuses to accept counterfeit. That this fundamental irony does not escape Danton's awareness is reflected in his words to Marion at the end of the scene: "To lose so much time! That was worth the effort!"[22] A temporary illusion is better than no illusion at all, but since its lack of permanence is preconditioned by the necessary intrusion of a sharply contrasting reality, its effect represents nothing but a loss of time.

The idea that "loss of time" nevertheless constitutes the desired result of concentrated efforts means, in effect, that nothingness, i.e., lack of awareness, is preferable to any imaginable confrontation with reality. In other words, Danton's pursuit of pleasure, which could, at best, lead to strictly limited moments of euphoria, offers him only a most precarious foothold on life. Epicureanism falls far short of answering the plea of his intellect for a haven from awareness, which is implicit not only in the previously discussed opening lines of the drama, but in all his actions and thoughts.

On the one hand, the bordello scene shows the desperation in Danton's attempt to maintain this one foothold on life, while on the other hand, it relates directly to his external conflict with Robespierre. It is strategically placed directly before the climactic scene which offers the only confrontation between these two chief adversaries. Its obvious purpose is to give unequivocal substance to Robespierre's charge: "He wants to bring the horses of the Revolution to a halt at the bordello."[23] Again the juxtaposition of scenes places Robespierre in the best possible light and indicates Büchner's concern for historical objectivity.

Nevertheless, Danton dominates the discussion, for it very soon becomes apparent that while Robespierre with his moral pronouncements invokes an image of man as he should or must be in order to make a political system function, Danton is the spokesman for man as he is by nature—an individual with weaknesses and strengths which cannot easily be distinguished and, most important of all, with a great variation of desires: ". . . All men are epicureans, either crude or refined, as the case may be: Christ was the most refined of them all. That is the only difference that I can discern between men. Every man acts according to his own nature, that is, he does what does him good."[24] The whole German dramatic tradition since the advent of the Storm and Stress stands behind Danton's defense of the individual and against Robespierre's cold formulations, which are little more than variations of a single idea: "Vice must be punished."[25] But the importance of the scene goes beyond the reinforcement of already established sympathies toward the two adversaries or the restatement of Danton's views.

Indeed, this scene holds a crucial key for the understanding of the drama in that it shows that the inner forces which destroy Danton threaten every man, even Robespierre himself. As soon as Robespierre is left alone, it becomes clear that Danton's provocations have hit the mark. Danton's words—"Isn't there something inside you that whispers sometimes, quietly, secretly, that you lie, Robespierre, you lie?"[26]—lead to an inner dialogue which offers the only insight into Robespierre's psyche within the framework of the drama: ". . . It keeps coming back to me. Why can't I rid myself of these thoughts? He [Danton] points his bloody finger at me here, here! I can wrap it in as many bandages as I like, but blood will always come through. . . . I don't know which part of me is lying to the other. . . ."[27] Since Büchner avoids a full characterization of Robespierre, this glimpse of his inner world—especially because it could be regarded as a flaw in the otherwise purely historical approach to this figure—can be expected to have a special bearing upon Danton's tragedy—the main concern of the drama.

The sudden revelation that, despite his firm political stance,

Robespierre is a man torn asunder with insoluble inner conflicts not only shows that Danton is right in the assessment of his adversary but also gives substance to the conviction that an individual's only chance for survival is to escape from the world of reality into one of illusion. Robespierre has no difficulty in functioning in the world which fits his pat formulations. But the moment his confrontation with Danton forces him into a critical self-assessment he is filled with doubts. When he asks himself which part of him is lying to the other, he is, in effect, admitting the existence of a reality which has no relationship whatever to his image of himself. At least for a moment he is troubled by the possibility that the world which requires him to act the role of a moral paragon—a world in which concepts such as "Virtue must rule through Terror" become a social necessity, and one in which a man like Danton represents a threat to be eliminated—is nothing but a fantasy generated by the mind: "Is our waking anything but a dream, a clear dream? Are we not all sleepwalkers? What are our actions but the actions of a dream, only more clear, more definite, more complete?" These are the questions which suddenly haunt him.

That Robespierre comes remarkably close to Danton when he directs his thoughts inward is self-evident from these questions. The only real difference is that Robespierre never goes beyond their mere formulation, while Danton, as the first scene of the drama has already shown, sees the meaninglessness of all human activity reflected in the conclusion toward which they point: that it is impossible to distinguish between dream—or illusion—and reality. Actually, Robespierre's sudden fear of the darkness hints that he is dangerously close to drawing the same conclusion; but his perilous speculations are cut short by the appearance of Saint-Just, whose political pragmatism restores Robespierre's composure. Indeed, Saint-Just intoxicates him with such self-confidence that all his doubts seem to vanish. Again he sees himself as the great savior of mankind:

ROBESPIERRE [alone]: Yes, [I am] the bloody Messiah who sacrifices himself but will not himself be sacrificed. He redeemed them with His blood, and I will redeem them with their own. He created them sinners, and I take the sin on myself. He suffered the ecstasy of pain, and I the torment of the executioner. Who denied himself, He or I?[28]

Objectively, Robespierre's "waking" is indeed a dream, and the world in which he casts himself in the role of a new and greater Messiah must be a world of his own fantasy. Büchner's message seems clear. The capacity for self-deception, lacking in Danton, is the essential ingredient of purposeful human action. The greatest danger to both man and his endeavors is the constant possibility of a genuine awakening. To emphasize this danger, Büchner gives Robespierre yet another brief moment of disillusioning insight at the very end of the scene. The Messianic image of himself, so essential to his mission, is not altogether safely entrenched. Renewed doubts shake its very foundation: ". . . yet there is something foolish in the thought of being the bloody Messiah. . . . They are all leaving me—the world is empty and void—I am alone." Robespierre totters at the brink of precisely the same abyss which engulfs Danton. Whether he loses his foothold is not an issue in the drama. But the fact that the historical Robespierre became a victim of his own death machine after he himself had appealed to the Convention for an end to the Reign of Terror, following Danton to the guillotine by less than four months, is certainly brought to mind at this point.

Actually, Büchner's Robespierre does not seem to be totally unconscious of the danger of becoming another Danton. Although his denunciation of the Dantonists before the National Convention is his only further appearance in the drama, one sentence from that speech does take on special meaning in relation to his inner conflict: "And so I declare this to you: . . . nothing will blunt my purpose; even though Danton's danger become my own."[29] Ostensibly this refers to Robespierre's fearlessness in the face of physical danger, but since the statement itself raises the issue of undeterring resolve—the very quality which the previously discussed scene puts into doubt—it would also seem to express his determination not to lose his fervor as a revolutionary. After all, Danton's danger, according to the charges of moderationism against him, stems from the loss of political fervor. Therefore, Robespierre's Danton-like inner threat is revealed to the audience. Since, at the same time, Büchner characterizes him as a man who allows the outer world to see nothing but total dedication to moral and political dogma, a double purpose is accomplished. First of all, the universality of Danton's condition is underscored by the revelation that even the most ardent dogmatist is susceptible. Secondly, the very substance of all dogmas, even those which prove responsive to political necessities, is challenged. The contrast between Robespierre's external certainty and his inner doubts, in other words, offers dramatic proof of Danton's fatal conclusion that man's inability to distinguish illusion from reality makes all human endeavors pointless or, to state the same conclusion once more in the terms of Robespierre's inner voice, "our actions are but the actions of a dream."

Man's tragic flaw, according to *Danton's Death*, lies in the mind, which has the dangerous potential of penetrating the veil of life-supporting illusions and of exposing the consciousness to a barren world of reality in which all values, including life and death, vanish. Under such conditions, only those individuals who lack the power or the will to see through their delusions can lead so-called normal, productive lives. In other words, what is usually meant by the term *sanity* reveals itself, within the drama, to be a kind of commonplace insanity, hardly distinguishable from what is usually meant by the term insanity. The idea that normality and madness are only varying degrees of the same human quality is clearly expressed by Camille, who once more echoes Danton's often expressed, but less directly formulated, views: "The usual kind of *idée fixe*, to which we have given the name common sense, is unbearably boring. The only way to be happy is to imagine oneself to be Father, Son and Holy Ghost all in one."[30] The only difference Camille sees between normality and the most extreme of possible delusions is that the former leads to boredom, while the latter is happiness.

The dramatic treatment of the idea that so-called sanity is actually a mass psychosis offers unique structural challenges. The traditional dramatic form uses monologue and dialogue to unveil and demonstrate "truth." Since the only "truth" to be revealed in *Danton* is that reality and truth cannot be recognized, the traditional forms are obviously inadequate. Rather than making theories and ideas credible, Büchner's theme requires him to cast doubt upon their validity even while they are being formulated. Whatever makes sense in a particular context must reveal itself to be invalid when held up against differing criteria. Thus when Robespierre, for example, expresses the idea that law is "the will of the people," an idea which is a cornerstone of democracy and seems to have political validity, it is simultaneously exposed as an absurdity against the background of the people's shout: "there is no more law." Likewise, the Dantonists' political theories based upon the doctrine of individualism, no matter how appealing, reveal themselves to be just as absurd in their exaggerated idealism when seen in juxtaposition to the exploitation of the economic plight of the poor.

Not just an arbitrary stylistic innovation, the collage-like structure of *Danton*, with its many short and seemingly fragmentary scenes, directly responds to the special requirements of the theme. Rather than offering a moral, political, or social doctrine, Büchner pieces together a panorama consisting of common moral, political, and social doctrines in such a way that in the absence of a resolution they are, in effect, cancelled out.

This method is perhaps most transparent in the first scene of Act III, where political prisoners discuss the question of the existence of God. The conversation is stimulated by Chaumette's fears in the face of death: ". . . help me a little with some of your argument," he pleads with Paine.[31] This plea in itself has an ironic effect, for it quickly becomes apparent that the spiritual comfort sought is the reassurance that God does not exist. Chaumette's plea shows that he already knows Paine's "arguments"; he merely wants to hear them again to fortify himself against recurrent doubts. The scene presents an inversion of a common, highly traditional motif, but the mocking tone with which Paine introduces his "catechism" of atheism is an immediate indication that his theological arguments are not to be taken altogether seriously:

PAINE: All right, Anaxagoras, I'll help you with your catechism. There is no God, because: either God created the world or He did not. If He did not, then the world contains its own first principle, and there is no God because God can only be God insofar as He contains the first principle of all things. . . .

This is the beginning of a lengthy exercise in pre-Kantian "reasoning" leading to the conclusion: ". . . it therefore follows that there can be no God. *Quod erat demonstrandum.*" But Büchner does not rely entirely upon the critical sense of his audience to recognize the fallaciousness of Paine's "proof," for no sooner concluded it is effectively negated by Hérault's even more transparent sophistry: "But my good Anaxagoras, one might also say: since God is all things, then He must also be his own opposite, that is perfect and imperfect, good and evil, happy and unhappy; the result, of course, would be nil; each side would cancel out the other; we would come to nothing." Added to Paine's arguments, Hérault's thoughts serve to allay Chaumette's fears, a fact which heightens the grotesquely comic effect of the scene but, since the premises are mutually exclusive, voids it of serious theological significance. A God who cancels himself out also cancels out Paine's "proof."

The fact that conflicting systems are left unresolved does not mean that the scene is devoid of dramatic meaning. On the contrary, this scene again points directly to the main theme of the drama: the gap between human conception of reality and reality itself. Despite its capacity to perceive, think, reason, and believe, the mind is not capable of bridging this gap; it is not capable of knowing. Perhaps this key idea is most directly expressed in Hérault's prefacing remark, "one might also say . . . ," which shows a considerable respect for the possible difference between what might be reasonable and what is true.

Büchner's purpose in this scene, as in others, is to bring widely accepted dogmas into the perspective of complete skepticism. The skepticism is not limited to throwing doubt upon the represented ideas alone—i.e., the belief in the existence of God—it actually turns back upon itself and, in effect, casts doubt upon its own disbelief. In other words, Büchner attempts to sketch the world from the same disjointed, pernicious perspective which carries Danton to tragedy.

Danton's own speculations on atheism, which occur a few scenes later, amplify the lack of resolution which this perspective of skepticism forces upon the mind. In distinct contrast to Paine, Danton cannot create a catechetic haven for himself. Since he is incapable of "faith," the idea of God and the idea of Nothingness become equally meaningless to him:

PHILIPPEAU: Then what do you want?
DANTON: Peace.
PHILIPPEAU: Peace is in God.
DANTON: Peace is in nothingness. Sink yourself into something more peaceful than nothingness, and if the ultimate peace is God, then God must be nothingness. However, I'm an atheist. Damn whoever said:

Danton's Death

Something cannot become nothing! The pitiable fact is that I am something! Creation has spread itself so far that there is nothing empty anymore, multitudes everywhere. This is the suicide of nothingness, creation is its wound, we its drops of blood, and the world its grave in which it rots. Mad as that sounds, there is some truth in it.[32]

Büchner's unorthodox dramatic structure, with its all but endless series of unresolved points and counterpoints, is aimed at making this kind of "mad-sounding" conjecture reveal the "truth" it contains. Danton's incapacity for faith, the rebellion of his mind not only against arbitrarily established dogmas but also against its own formulations, is no more than a reflection of the intellectual chaos with which Büchner surrounds him. The seemingly irreconcilable rejection of both God and Nothingness is the only consistent response to the disintegrated image of the world confronting the audience as well as Danton himself.

In *Danton*, form and content fuse to focus upon the idea that the fundamental basis for tragedy lies not within man but in the outside world. Büchner's drama could be called the tragedy of the sound mind operating in a chaotic environment. The sounder the mind, the less it can cope with that environment—the less it can comprehend that which is incomprehensible. From the very beginning of the drama, Danton is victimized by the fractured image of a world, the jagged fissures of which increase in magnitude and complexity the more closely they are observed.

Seeming inconsistencies in Danton's actions, which have generated considerable debate among critics—for example, Danton's belated, half-hearted attempt to defend himself before the Revolutionary Tribunal[33]—become unproblematic if the nature of the tragedy is understood. Throughout the drama, Danton is confronted by a choice between life and death. While it is clear from the first that Danton is doomed unless he acts, several courses of action to save himself seem to be open for him. But the fact that he does not act swiftly does not automatically mean a choice in favor of death; nor do his impassioned speeches to the Tribunal indicate a clear decision to live. In an ordered world, the choice—and hence the course of action—might be determined by relative values—positive or negative. But it is precisely the point of the drama that Danton, whose world lacks all semblance of order, has no basis for making decisions. "There is no hope in death," he says, "it's only a less complicated form of decay than

[47]

life—that's the only difference!"[34] Decisiveness on this most crucial question would actually be a most serious inconsistency of character. A mind driven to a nihilism so extreme that it even rejects the idea of nothingness ("If only we could believe in annihilation!"[35]) is a mind of endless ambiguities which can only express itself through paradoxes such as: "Of course it's miserable having to die. What does death do but mimic birth?"[36]

CHAPTER 3

Lenz

The Edge of Insanity

THE idea for a work based on the life of the German dramatist and lyric poet Jacob Michael Reinhold Lenz (1751–92)
might well date back to Büchner's first visit to Strasbourg (1831–
33), although there is no indication that he wrote any part of it
before 1835. The obvious source for *Lenz* was the diary-like report of Pastor Johann Friedrich Oberlin (1740–1826), at whose
house in the little Alsatian town of Waldbach in Steinthal Lenz
had spent a few weeks early in 1778, in the hope of overcoming
the effects of severe schizophrenic attacks. Oberlin's papers fell
into Büchner's hands through his student friend August Stöber,
who himself had written an essay on the Oberlin-Lenz relationship in 1831.[1]

There are good reasons for Büchner's great interest in Lenz.
First of all, a renewed general interest in this poet, whose contri-
bution as a creative writer to the Storm and Stress movement
must be considered second only to Goethe's, was fanned by the
appearance of the first collected edition of his works during
Büchner's last school years.[2] Judging from the style of *Danton*,
Lenz's stormy dramas with their many, often disjointed themes,
which he called "comedies" despite their bitter and often tragic
content, must have had a special appeal for Büchner. Furthermore, Lenz's lifelong bout with madness certainly attracted Büchner's scientific curiosity as well as his personal sympathy. *Danton*,
after all, proves Büchner's fascination with all matters pertaining
to the mind and its functions, including the question of insanity.
The scientific research which led to the writing of the two treat-
ises, "On the Nervous System of the Barbel," and "On the Cranial
Nerves" shows that Büchner's interest in the nervous system was
neither casual nor purely speculative. In fact, it would hardly be
an exaggeration to recognize a driving preoccupation here. Büch-

ner's professional interests, both as a writer and as a scientist, quite naturally converged upon the figure of Lenz.

But Lenz aroused more than purely professional curiosity in Büchner. Even the most casual reading of Büchner's only narrative work reveals a measure of understanding and sympathy so deep that a strong emotional attachment becomes evident. It seems quite possible, even likely, that there was a great deal of self-identification involved in Büchner's feeling toward Lenz. Certainly there are some striking similarities in their lives. Like Büchner, Lenz had been a frail but extremely precocious individual. Just sixty years before Büchner, he had arrived in Strasbourg and joined the radical student circles of that day. He was soon accepted into the inner core of the Herder-Goethe group which represented the nucleus of the Storm and Stress movement. However, it is evident from various accounts, notably Goethe's memoirs,[3] that, while Lenz found recognition and even admiration for his talent, his personality evidently evoked little warmth from others.[4]

Büchner's own problems of this nature have already been discussed. He, too, felt the anguish of rejection when he wrote to his fiancée from Giessen: "My friends are all deserting me."[5] It is noteworthy at least in passing that, during the extreme mental crisis of this period following his attack of meningitis, he ended a letter meant to console Wilhelmine with what he called an "ancient lullaby"—actually, lines from a poem by Lenz devoted to his gentle, yet unrequited, love for the daughter of a country pastor (presumably Friederike Brion) who cannot forget the man (Goethe) who "took her heart when she was but a child."[6] To be sure, Büchner radically changed the meaning of the poem by selecting only a few lines portraying the girl's silent suffering after the departure of her secret lover, but there is some reason to suspect that even in his love for the daughter of Pastor Jaegle he felt a sort of kinship with Lenz. The fact that he concealed the source of the verses from Wilhelmine only tends to support this suspicion.

The idea that Büchner might have considered his collapse in Giessen—which, by his own account, left him in a dimly brooding darkness for days and brought him night after night of feverish restlessness—to be a danger signal of an impending Lenz-like fate would be pure conjecture; yet the constant recurrence of the theme of madness in all his literary works allows at least the possibility that he harbored such fears.

Lenz's fate was tragic, indeed. Friendless, barred from intellectual and social circles because of his sporadic attacks of schizophrenia, all but forgotten by his former companions, and exiled by his family, he spent the last twelve years of his life isolated in Russia, toward the end enjoying only rare lucid intervals. He died in Moscow at the age of forty-one, having found but little understanding and nothing that might be called love. But Büchner brought to the image of the poet Lenz some of the warmth which had been denied to the man. In his *Lenz*, he presents to the world a man whose every gesture he reads, whose every expression he understands, whose agony, joy, fear, and hope he knows—in short, he presents a man whose tender but fragile spirit has captivated him.

Büchner's *Lenz* has little in common with the novels and novellas dealing with the life and problems of the artist which were so much in vogue in Germany throughout the nineteenth century. It has even less in common with the sensationalism which, traditionally, dominated works exploring the question of insanity. In fact it would be difficult to categorize *Lenz* in any way, since it stands quite outside the German narrative tradition. If anything, it represents an even more radical departure than *Danton*.

From the point of view of nineteenth-century literary concepts, the most striking feature of *Lenz* is its weak, almost nonexistent plot. Action is rarely the focal point; and even when it is treated in some detail, a feeling of nonchalance prevails. Events are reported in an undramatic, matter-of-fact, and often telegraphic style with a disregard for chronological and topical sequence. Frequently, the narrative only summarizes action; that is, instead of telling precisely what happens, the narrator offers only a brief sketch, as in the following passage: "Inside the huts there was lively activity: they thronged around Oberlin; he admonished, gave advice, consoled; everywhere trusting glances, prayer. The people told about dreams, premonitions. Then quickly, back to the practical life: Laying out roads, digging canals, going to school."[7] A whole range of events is here concentrated into a few sentences. The language is cut to the bone, in an effort to achieve the greatest possible economy. Verbs and conjunctions are omitted, and hours are compressed into single phrases. Although

GEORG BÜCHNER

not all action scenes are as abbreviated as this one, it is characteristic for Büchner's studied inclination to minimize the importance of action.

Even more important to the structure of the narrative is the lack of connection between the various bits of "plot." Instead of giving a sense of continuity to the work, fragments of action tend rather to stress the often abrupt shifts in direction. Occasionally, such shifts even occur in the middle of a sentence, as in the following case: "Lenz went to his room pleased. He thought of a text for his sermon and lost himself in contemplation, and his nights became quiet."[8] After a relatively detailed description of a conversation between Oberlin and Lenz, which precedes the quoted passage, a single sentence brings the evening's activities to an end and, with the interposition of a comma, lunges an unspecified number of days ahead. To be sure, the sentence does, in a way, connect two phases, but the connection does no more than underscore the gap by calling attention to it.

Other gaps are more conventionally bridged. When actions or ideas are interrupted, a new paragraph is introduced with a— sometimes precise and sometimes vague—time reference such as, *On the third of February, The next day, A few days later, One morning*—phrases which are used with astonishing frequency. Superficially, these, too, are connective. Actually, they signal a programmatic effort on the part of Büchner to break the continuum of action into a series of separate scenes, most of which are not properly linked. Only the fact that they all deal with the same figure, Lenz, gives the work an overall sense of unity.

The lack of continuity in the action is matched by an equally studied fragmentation in the realm of ideas. Theological, esthetic, and mystical notions are presented in the form of more or less extensive fragments of conversation, some of which are reported in detail. Yet they are scattered in such a way as to suggest anything but a systematic approach. To be sure, a feeling for Lenz's *Weltanschauung* develops, but Büchner is more concerned with keeping it from causing a distraction than with formulating clear concepts. Just like the action sequences, strings of ideas are sometimes abbreviated and cut off abruptly in order to reduce their weight:

He [Lenz] expressed himself further. He said that each thing possessed its own inexpressible harmony . . . that higher forms with more organs were able to better choose, to express, to understand, and were therefore more deeply affected; and that lower forms were more repressed, more restricted, and therefore enjoyed a greater degree of tranquillity. He pursued his line of thought further, but Oberlin put an end to it because it led him too far afield from his simple ideas.[9]

Reminiscent of Goethe's biologically oriented philosophical speculations, Lenz here begins to develop a system of thought apparently aimed at relating certain psychological phenomena to the biological complexity of each organism. That such ideas touch close to the center of Büchner's intellectual interests can be seen from the fact that, in the heated attack upon the teleological approach to biology which serves as an introduction to his anatomical study, "On the Cranial Nerves," he invokes much the same premise about the inner harmony of all living beings, in which he discerns the operation of a single fundamental law.[10] The speculative extension of this life-governing law into the realm of psychology could certainly be expected to show some signs of deep personal involvement. Yet, despite the fact that the ideas have clearly captivated Lenz's imagination, they are left dangling in mid-air. Not only that; Büchner further underscores the relative lack of substantive importance in the arguments by adding the clause: "He pursued his line of thought further," thus, in effect, driving home the message that, while there is more to the argument, the whole thing is hardly worth reporting. A better way of undermining the ideas is hardly conceivable! But Büchner goes even one step further in his attempt to distract the reader's attention from the intellectual content of the story. He points out that such abstractions are really beyond the capacities and interests of a simple man like Oberlin. He thereby creates a radical shift in perspective, and the whole passage is seen in a different light. Suddenly it appears as if Lenz's line of thought had only been recorded to document the great intellectual gulf between the young poet and his host.

That Büchner gives such seemingly indifferent treatment even to those ideas which lie close to the center of his own interests can only be explained as resulting from overriding esthetic considerations. His methodical refusal to buttress continuity either with action or with a systematic train of thought represents a radical departure from narrative traditions. The important questions, of course, are not *whether* the narrative represents a formal rebellion or even *how* it does so; they are, rather, *why* did Büchner strike out in new directions, and precisely *what* were his esthetic aims?

Fortunately, Büchner facilitates the search for answers to these questions by offering a number of direct hints about his artistic goals within the text. Indeed, his most formidable statement on the nature and purpose of art is contained in *Lenz*. Perhaps *concealed* would be a better term, for the substance of the dialogue which yields the crucial ideas also bears the narrator's usual tone of disdain for such matters. This dialogue, too, is left hanging in the air in such a way as to make it seem that the narrator had anything but a burning interest in it. Again a simple statement— "He continued speaking in this manner"—[11] cuts the subject off with one blow and, at the same time, indicates the narrator's impatience to get on with more important things.

Understated as they are, the contents of this dialogue are nevertheless described at sufficient length to offer at least a starting point for understanding the esthetic basis of the novel approach represented by *Lenz*. There can be no doubt that the esthetic theories attributed to Lenz are Büchner's own, for there is not the slightest hint of such topics to be found in Oberlin's account, nor is there anything in Lenz's own esthetic writings which could have been used as a source. Büchner, on the other hand, applied some of the same arguments—partially verbatim—to form the theoretical backbone for a defense of *Danton* against charges of indecency in a letter to his parents.[12] But the most convincing evidence is the narrative structure of *Lenz* itself, which clearly represents an attempt to put theory into practice.

The discussion takes place between Lenz and his friend Kaufmann, whose role is limited to that of a kind of straight man, that is, he represents common, rather philistine views against which Lenz then directs his attack. It is Kaufmann who raises the subject during a dinner conversation by declaring his adherence to the latest literary vogue:

The period of idealism was then in fashion, and Kaufmann was its disciple. Lenz spoke violently against it. He said that those poets who claimed to represent reality hadn't even a conception of it; nonetheless they are more bearable than those who want to glorify reality. He said that the good Lord had indeed made the world as it should be, and we ought not to think ourselves capable of improving upon it; our sole endeavor should be to imitate Him a bit.[13]

Lenz's two-pronged attack upon literary trends hits hardest against what is called the "period of idealism." The actual target is the esthetic tradition associated with Schiller (1759–1805). That point is clarified by the previously mentioned defense of *Danton*, where Büchner, using substantially the same argument, does not hesitate to call the devil by name. For the sake of at least a semblance of historical accuracy, Schiller could not be mentioned in *Lenz*, since he did not appear on the literary scene until several years after 1778. Yet the omission of the name can hardly obliterate the anachronism of the argument itself which, more properly, fits into Büchner's own time—a time that, as he might have expressed it, still suffered from the excessive weight of Schiller's influence.

The inclusion of such an attack on Schiller in *Lenz* runs directly counter to Büchner's conception of the poet as an historian who simply "creates history for the second time."[14] In other words, the anachronism offered good reasons for hesitation. The fact that Büchner nevertheless included it shows that he must have considered it crucially important—so important, in fact, that he was willing to sacrifice one of his fundamental esthetic principles for it. Indeed, the very words Büchner attributes to Lenz inveigh against the falsification of reality, and it must be assumed that he would include historical reality. What, then, could justify this perhaps minor but nonetheless conscious bit of historical falsification? Certainly nothing short of the firm conviction that the work as a whole, or at least its central idea, needed that kind of clarification which could only be purchased at the expense of absolute historical integrity.

In terms of the theme of *Lenz* (a young man's battle against madness), an attack upon idealism in literature, or any other esthetic argument, hardly seems crucial enough to warrant a compromise of principle. The previously discussed technique of de-emphasis in the realm of ideas, after all, shows that in terms of the theme, Büchner did not consider the episode to be exceptionally important. It therefore seems likely that with the Lenz-Kaufmann dialogue Büchner wanted to throw light not upon the content but upon the form of the work, and perhaps upon the relationship between form and content.

Actually, the previously quoted passage constitutes more than a mere attack upon idealism. Those who "claim to represent reality" but fail to do so are hardly spared. The important problem raised is the general failure of poets to come to terms with reality. Some fail because they have no true conception of it, others because they consciously turn away from it. It is quite natural that the latter bear the brunt of the criticism, for they are the ones who methodically destroy what is given as the first and only principle of art: "to imitate Him a bit." Nevertheless, the productions of both groups, as is pointed out a few lines later, are rejected as equally worthless. In effect, this amounts to a summary rejection of literary tradition. Subsequently, only Shakespeare, some passages in Goethe, and folk ballads are excepted from the condemnation.

If he wishes to come to terms with reality, the poet must absolutely restrict himself to the "sole endeavor" of imitating nature (God-made reality). This is the heart of the argument. Everything else is only an elaboration of this idea. Taken literally, it means that literature is limited to descriptive techniques which have the sole aim of reproducing the likeness of life. When he continues the discussion, Büchner-Lenz goes on to explain how he thinks the artist should proceed. Notably, there is no differentiation between the various media of art:

I demand of art that it be life . . . nothing else matters; we then have no need to ask whether it is beautiful or ugly. . . . These people can't so much as draw a dog's kennel. They try to create ideal forms, but all I have seen of their work looks more like wooden dolls. Let them try just once to immerse themselves in the life of humble people and then reproduce this again in all its movements, its implications, in its subtle, scarcely discernible play of expressions.

"Life," as Büchner uses the term here, obviously does not mean biography. It refers to those inner forces which constitute the essence of being. What happens to people, where they go, and what they do, is of artistic importance only insofar as it represents an outward expression of these forces. Life reveals itself through the silent language of precisely such expressions—Büchner calls it "a scarcely discernible play of expression"—, and it should be the artist's exclusive aim to translate this language into poetry, painting, or sculpture. To accomplish this he must first immerse himself in the life of others, so that he will understand even the finest subtleties and nuances. Ordinary people are portrayed as the best models because their simple ways offer the most direct access to the essence of life which, as Büchner himself goes on to point out, is to be found in the "organs of feeling." These, he claims, "are the same in almost all men; the only difference is the thickness of the crust through which we must break."

Only when the artist has immersed himself in the life of the people, when he has broken through the crust and exposed the organs of feeling to view, and when he has learned to read the language of wordless expression, should he turn to the technical problem of reproduction; and Büchner also makes himself quite clear as to the guiding principle of this last step in the creative process. He circumscribes this principle by means of a symbol (Lenz is still speaking):

As I walked in the valley yesterday I saw two girls sitting on a rock; one of them was binding up her hair, and the other helped her with it. Her golden hair hung down, her face serious and pale and young, her dress was black, and the other girl so attentive to help her. . . . One might wish at times to be a Medusa's head, so as to be able to transform such a group into stone and summon the world to see it. Then they rose, and the beautiful grouping was destroyed; but as they descended between the rocks they formed another picture.

The Medusa's head, with its power to turn living beings into stone, obviously is meant as a symbol for the highest aspirations of the artist. Perfection in art is represented by an exact but frozen image of life. While this conception is primarily a somewhat amplified echo of the previously expressed demand for the faithful reproduction of reality, it is rich in overtones. Particularly striking is the heavy emphasis it places upon the static nature of art. Büchner wants to leave no doubt that the Medusa's head symbolizes perfection in all mimetic arts, including literature, when, a few sentences later, he has Lenz point out the difficulty of holding such "pictures" in the mind and transferring them to paper. The very fact, then, that Büchner chooses to symbolize the transformation of life into art by creating a completely static ideal strongly suggests that he considers any attempt to capture movement or action by means of literary techniques as superfluous and unrelated to the essential qualities of art. In any case, applying the Medusa's head symbol to literature implies a direct rejection of the widespread, and generally accepted, view associated with Lessing, who in his *Laocoon* (1766), undoubtedly the most influential esthetic treatise coming out of eighteenth-century Germany, gave literature a privileged position among the arts, precisely because it has the unique power to portray movement in time.

Büchner, of course, does not argue with the fact that poetry can simulate the fluidity of life. What he does suggest is that there is, at best, only very limited value in this power. The last sentence of the above quotation recognizes the fact that a series of "pictures" can produce the feeling of temporal continuity in art; but, at the same time, it puts forward the idea that these pictures should not be brought into close contact with one another. In fact, the stress is on their clear demarcation. The first image of the girls sitting in a group is "destroyed" before the next, completely different one takes shape. The action connecting the two petrified moments apparently reveals nothing essential about "life." The unmistakable implication is that the power to penetrate the "crust" and reveal those inner forces to which the artist owes his full allegiance is vested solely in the frozen image.

Even more important is the closely associated implication that life itself gives expression to its essence only in motionless pictures. Indeed, this must be considered the guiding principle of the emerging conception of artistic form, for it gives a truly functional meaning to the basic esthetic tenet that "art be life." Not only is the content of the work of art to be limited to the realistic representation of life, but the form—the vehicle of artistic expression—must be dictated by the manner in which the inner forces of man come to be expressed. In other words, art must communicate in the same way in which life communicates. If the inner man breaks through the surface only in fleeting, all but timeless and motionless, configurations (and precisely this is Büchner's intimation), there is every reason for the artist to restrict himself to the portrayal of these instances, allowing "life" to express itself in its own language.

The literary form suggested by these considerations consists of static scenes or "pictures," each of which captures a revealing moment and then dissolves to make way for another. That such a chain of relatively independent images has no need for external unification is stressed once more when Lenz continues his argument: "The most beautiful pictures, the most swelling tones, form a group and then dissolve. Only one thing remains: an unending beauty which passes from one form to another, eternally revealed, eternally unchanged." The only necessary unifying force is the integrity of the individual scenes, for it is precisely the endless variation of the forms that unveils the eternally unchanging beauty inherent in the revelation of the inner spirit of man.

There can be no doubt that the narrative form of *Lenz* reflects the esthetic ideals set forth within the text. To be sure, the argument does not represent anything that might be called a systematic approach—in a way, more problems are raised than solved by it—but it does point to a number of priorities which quite obviously guided Büchner. Moreover, the definition of artistic aims within the work, even on a highly abstract level, actually makes its form thematic. *Lenz* is not only meant as a work of art in its own right, but also as a kind of working model demonstrating specific literary theories. On the one hand, the theory illuminates the artistic aims of the work; while at the same time, the work constitutes a practical application of the theory. For example, if applied to *Lenz*, the theory would seem to demand anything but the story of a young man's experiences: Like any "true" work of art, it should strictly limit itself to the portrayal of the inner forces of life. The very last sentence of the work calls special attention to the importance of exactly this limitation, thereby underscoring Büchner's overall aim: "So (in this way) his life went on."[15] In effect, this means: the portrait is complete, Lenz's "life" continues without change, regardless of where he goes or what happens to him; or, in terms of the theory, once the outer "crust" has been penetrated and the "organs of feeling" exposed, nothing else is of artistic significance. Just as the two girls, described by Lenz, walk out of their "picture" into an unknown future, leaving the spirit of their existence imprinted upon the artist's memory, so Lenz himself walks out of Büchner's completed narrative portrait of him.

While the theory elucidates the goals of the work, the work, in turn, defines its implications as it applies specifically to literature. Central among the theoretical principles is the demand for a rather complex relationship between artist and subject. The necessity for the self-immersion of the artist in his subject is juxtaposed with the seemingly conflicting demand for the cold objectivity of the Medusa's head. In purely theoretical terms, this represents a somewhat disturbing dichotomy. On the one hand, the artist must enter into the world of the subject's feelings, while on the other, he is obliged to remain a distant and uninvolved observer in order to avoid the danger of falsification. Turning to the text would seem to offer the most direct approach to a possible resolution. How did Büchner actually satisfy both of these divergent demands in his work?

Besides helping to explain the theory, the answer to this question throws light on one of the thorniest problems in *Lenz*. The nature and urgency of this problem is revealed in one of the most recent interpretations of the work where the author-subject relationship is summed up in one sentence: "The story is told from Lenz's point of view; although it is in the third person, we view the events almost wholly (but not quite) as Lenz sees them, without direct comment from the author."[16] Indeed, this is almost (but not quite) an accurate description of the point of view; but a fine distinction here means the difference between the success and the failure of Büchner's experiment. If Büchner really had wanted to tell the story from Lenz's point of view, he could hardly have chosen a less suitable vehicle than a straightforward third-person approach. It is fairly clear that the critic just quoted had certain misgivings about the apparent contradiction—between the first-person point of view and the third-person form—and rightly so. But there is yet another objection. A first-person point of view in the story would make the symbol of the Medusa's head into an empty slogan having no relation whatsoever to Büchner's own narrative style; to emulate the Medusa's head, the poet, at the very least, must keep his identity separate from that of his subject. Hence the question as to whether or not the story actually is told from Lenz's point of view is a crucial one, for if it is, the work would have to be condemned as clumsy and unsuccessful on at least two counts. Neither the choice of a fake third person nor the spinning of esthetic theories stressing the necessity for objectivity could be artistically justified. Yet, on a close reading of the text, it does almost seem as if the reader were seeing the world through Lenz's eyes. Almost, but not quite—and therein lies the vital, if hardly discernible, distinction. It is not that "we view the events almost wholly (but not quite) as Lenz sees them"; it is rather that the reader sees the events wholly from almost (but not quite) the same viewpoint as Lenz. Never does the author— or the reader—look at the world through the lenses of Lenz's eyes, but he repeatedly comes very close to doing that, so close, in fact, that, at times, only the relentless use of the third person form upholds the distinction.

To understand this distinction it is necessary to consider not only the point of view—that is, from what relative point the action is seen—but also the direction of the narrator's gaze. The Medusa's head directs its eyes toward the subject at all times, and never away, no matter how close to the subject it might be. Immersed in its subject, its eyes still would be directed toward the center and not toward the outside. This model defines quite precisely Büchner's relationship to his subject. Basically adopting a typical third-person narrative stance, he views Lenz from the outside. But frequently, after having given a picture of the outer reality, he immerses himself in Lenz's being. When he immerses himself in this way, he continues to direct his gaze toward the center of Lenz's inner world; he does not, so to speak, turn round and look back out through Lenz's eyes. To be sure, the outside world finds its reflection within—but only after the impressions have penetrated Lenz's consciousness, and have become part of his inner world. In other words, Büchner first describes Lenz and the people and objects around him as an outside observer might perceive them, and then he enters into Lenz's consciousness and records the latter's intellectual and emotional reactions to the aspects of reality he has described. Therefore, Lenz's actions are not seen in relation to his own, possibly erroneous and, in any case, subjective perceptions, but against a background of a reality as observed by the "objective" narrator.

Büchner's "pictures" of Lenz are, of course, not limited to visual impressions. Immersion in Lenz's inner world allows him to tune in on all sensations and feelings as well. The picture of this inner reality is no less objectively drawn than that of the outer realm. Büchner neither analyzes nor empathizes with his hero's mental responses; he simply describes them and allows them to communicate directly with the reader. The result is that the reader comes to understand and sympathize with Lenz but does not actually identify with him. Throughout the work, Lenz maintains his own clearly separate identity; he always remains a third person, not only in a grammatical, but also in a real, sense.

The opening passage of *Lenz* establishes just this kind of relationship between the reader and the protagonist. Büchner does not hesitate to use what might be called literary shock treatment to place the reader at the proper angle. Italics are used here to make the distinction between *inner* and outer reality graphically evident:

On the twentieth of January Lenz went through the mountains. The peaks and the high regions white with snow, down the valleys: gray stone, green surfaces, boulders and fir trees. It was damp and cold; the water rushed down the rocks and leaped over the road. The fir branches hung down heavily in the damp air. Gray clouds drifted across the sky, but everything so dense—and then the mist rose up from below and moved through the brush—so languidly, so heavily. *He walked on indifferently, the road meant nothing to him, sometimes uphill, then again downhill. He did not feel tired, only occasionally he regretted not being able to walk upside down.*[17]

Both in time and in space, the first glimpse of Lenz comes from a distance. While the actual date, January 20, agrees with historical fact, it is obviously not Büchner's intention to establish a true historical perspective. He makes no mention of the year. The yearless date does give an indication of the author's special interest in details, which contrasts strikingly with his disregard for the larger contexts. The same can be said about the mountainscape which, at first, dwarfs the walking figure. Its huge dimensions consist only of a rough interplay of color areas and vaguely defined objects. The supression of verbs accelerates the description and, at the same time, reduces the gap between the individual aspects of the image. The landscape is like a roughly sketched background in a painting; its functions are striking a mood and focusing attention upon the central subject. After the second sentence, the description proceeds beyond visual impressions. In remarkably few words, Büchner evokes all the feelings that make a mid-winter day a reality: coldness, dampness, oppressive closeness, languidness, heaviness of spirit. The scene is neither beautiful nor ugly. In fact, it is hardly a scene at all; it is more like a force impressing itself upon the reader's feelings, and as it presses in, the focus shifts to Lenz's inner reaction to that force. But the reader is in no way swept up in Lenz's feelings; he understands them, but does not share his response to the surroundings. Büchner creates a distance between his hero and the reader by eliciting an emotional response toward a winter mountain scene from the reader, a response that is totally different from that of his hero. Lenz feels indifferent toward the described landscape; he is only aware of the up and down of the road, but not of the snow and the water, the coldness and dampness, or the high peaks and the valleys below. Right from the beginning then, Büchner establishes for himself a clearly separate identity as a narrator who is aware of many things that escape the hero's notice. The distinction is reinforced when Büchner goes on to state what Lenz does not feel: "He did not feel tired." Except in memoirs, where the writer examines his own feelings at an earlier time, such an observation would hardly be valid in its first-person form. Only on very rare occasions does a person become aware of what he does not feel. But an objective recording device implanted in the nervous system (a kind of Medusa's head which freezes mental images) can reveal both what is, and also what is not, there.

By describing non-feelings along with feelings, Büchner throws the focus upon the often surprising transformation of outer reality into emotional response from the very beginning. In order to make his intention crystal clear, he chooses a particularly startling, highly irrational aberration in his opening "picture." Lenz's inner response to the sensations of a mid-winter day in the mountains is an occasional feeling of regret at not being able to walk upside down. To see the aberration requires a vantage point different, albeit only slightly so, from that of the man within whom it occurs. The stimulation of the nerve endings by what is actually there on the outside, and the emotional response to it, become separate entities in the reader's mind. In effect, the reader comes to know much more about Lenz than either Lenz, or the reader, could possibly know about himself, making true self-identification impossible.

Because of the irrationality of Lenz's response, the first "pic-

ture" fixes the author's—and also the reader's—perspective especially succinctly. Though the focus is always upon Lenz, the
point of view shifts freely from outside to inside. The author
looks at Lenz from a distance, sees him in his environment, and
then penetrates his emotional existence. There seem to be two
separate, well-defined levels of reality which might be identified
simply as outer and inner reality. Some other passages, however,
present a more complex structure. In these, three levels can be
distinguished. Between the outer level and the level of emotional or intellectual response, a third level, that of Lenz's perceptions, is interposed. The following is perhaps the most concentrated example; again the various levels are distinguished by
the use of varying print:

He went through the village. The lights shone through the windows,
he looked in while passing: CHILDREN SITTING AT THE TABLE,
OLD WOMEN, GIRLS, THEIR FACES CALM AND SERENE. *It
seemed to him the light streamed from their faces; his spirit was lightened, he was almost at the parsonage in Waldbach.*[18]

First Lenz is seen from the outside as he walks through the little village. Lights shining through the windows are only periph-
erally visible. Just as in the opening passage, the observer or
narrator keeps his eyes focused upon Lenz. But then the observer immerses himself within Lenz and describes those objects
within the scene which Lenz perceives. Lenz sees much more
detail because he is looking directly at the lighted windows while
the observer was looking at Lenz walking past the houses. However, not everything that is there for Lenz to see, but only those
details which strike his consciousness—the sitting children, the
serene faces of the old women and the girls—are recorded. Finally, the perceptions are transformed into psychological responses; the observer now examines Lenz's emotions, which
reflect not only his perceptions but also his intellect. Lenz knows
that the lighted windows signal the proximity of his goal. The
perceptions are interpreted in terms of this knowledge and translated into emotional reality: His spirit is lightened; he finds release from the anxieties that had previously plagued him.
    The dimensions of Lenz's inner world are put in perspective
by the juxtaposition of the various levels. In fact, it is this three-

dimensional representation of reality which allows Büchner to dispense with explanations and analyses of his hero's thoughts and behavior, even though the central issue of the work is the psychology of madness. Again and again, the reader is confronted with a scene or event witnessed by both Lenz and the narrator, whose eyes never stray away from Lenz. The narrator then pursues the effect of the scene or event into the realm of Lenz's consciousness, where its perception and mental impact become matters of simple description. Sometimes the observer moves in and out several times in a single passage. While the process of shifting from one level to another gives a certain perspective of depth, it also necessitates the sacrifice of close chronological continuity both in the representation of actions and in the realm of ideas. Pursuing a complex series of actions through all three levels of reality would be laborious if not impossible. Hence Büchner's conception that literature, like painting and sculpture, should consist of relatively static and independent "pictures" might well spring, at least in part, from the necessities imposed by his particular conception of the narrative structure. The attempt to capture a complex, closely integrated sequence in time and space on three levels at once would at best lead to the kind of wordiness very much at odds with Büchner's obvious taste for simplicity and directness.

Of course, Büchner does not altogether dispense with the representation of actions, but he does limit strict chronological sequences to very short periods of time. An examination of precisely those passages which seem to be most oriented toward action offers perhaps the best method of demonstrating just how the concern for depth dominates his style, for it is in these that the maintenance of several levels creates the greatest technical problems. Without question, the most extensively detailed and vivid action sequence in the work is the following:

Finally it was time to leave. Because the parsonage was too small, they took him across the road and gave him a room in the schoolhouse. He went upstairs. IT WAS COLD UP THERE; A WIDE ROOM THAT WAS EMPTY, WITH A HIGH BED IN THE BACKGROUND. He placed the lamp on the table and paced back and forth. *He thought again about the day just past, how he had come here, where he was. The room in the parsonage with its lights and dear faces seemed like a shadow now, like a dream, and he felt empty again, as on the mountain; but he could not fill this emptiness with anything.* The light was out, darkness swallowed up all things. *He felt gripped by an unnamable fear.* He leaped from bed, ran down the stairs to the front of the house; *but all in vain,* EVERYTHING WAS DARK, *nothing—he himself was a dream. Isolated thoughts rushed through his mind; he held fast to them. It seemed he should be always repeating the "Lord's Prayer." He was lost; an obscure instinct drove him to save himself.* He thrust himself against the stones, he tore himself with his nails; *the pain began, bringing him to his senses.* He threw himself into the fountain but the water wasn't deep, he splashed about.[19]

Again, the observer initially views the subject from the outside. Although the individual images, even in the first few sentences, are too widely spaced to give the sequence real moment-to-moment fluidity, compared to other, far more static scenes, they do present a fairly smooth continuum of action until the instant Lenz reaches his room. At that point, there is the first shift of levels. The room, presumably, is described as Lenz perceives it. Then, in rapid succession, there are a number of shifts from one level to another, the primary stress being, throughout, on the innermost one. Perception is translated into desperation and terror and ultimately expresses itself in renewed action. While there is an overall chronological integration, there is a certain loss of continuity at each level. For example, on the outer level, Lenz's pacing back and forth is followed by his jumping from the bed, leaving an obvious gap in the narrative sequence. The important question, however, concerns the literary effect of the passage as a whole. How is the reader's reaction altered by the introduction of the deeper strata?

The climax of the action, particularly the image of the shallow fountain with Lenz splashing about, confronts the reader with an absurdity, which, indeed, the whole sequence of actions strains to produce. Yet, the interposing of the inner levels does not allow the humor attaching itself to the image (pathetic as it might be) to be fully exploited. The effect would be far more dramatic if the whole scene were viewed from the outside: Lenz puts the lamp on the table, paces back and forth; then the lamp goes out, he leaps out of bed, runs down the stairs; outside he hurls himself against the stones, tears himself with his nails, throws himself into the fountain: the water is shallow, he splashes about. Actually the pathos of the passage would not be seriously affected, while the comic effect would be greatly heightened by allowing for an emotional release. The surprising, rather ludicrous image of a man splashing about in a village fountain in the middle of a winter night would be augmented by the feelings of relief resulting from the awareness that there is no immediate danger in the situation. The inner dimension, however, stands diametrically opposed to this comic effect. Not only does the understanding of the inner motivation overshadow the sense of relief with the realization of the self-destructive forces lurking inside, but it also minimizes the surprise element. The sequence of actions takes on the appearance of an almost reasonable response to the inner distress. What is so distinctly the climax of the outer action, due to the deeper insight, becomes a relatively anticlimactic, strictly momentary, resolution of a much more ominous, inner crisis.

Without doubt, Büchner's multi-leveled perspective tends to subdue even violent, relatively impulsive action. It clearly does not offer the best vehicle for capturing the sheer drama of human action, and, of course, that is hardly the aim of the few action sequences in *Lenz*. On the contrary, it seems to be Büchner's purpose to counteract sensationalism without going so far as to deny the existence of the sensational. By superimposing the inner world upon the outer, he brings the reader face to face with terror in such a way that it hardly terrorizes, and with the comic in such a way that it has little comic effect. Neither is the reader drawn emotionally into Lenz's existence (Lenz's fear, in the absence of a genuine external cause, inspires sympathy but not fear), nor is he alienated by the absurdities to which Lenz's life exposes him. A delicate balance keeps attention focused on the real problem. Even the action scenes are aimed at defining what Lenz is, not what he does.

In every detail *Lenz* is so structured as to force the reader's attention away from external appearances and toward the inner reality of existence. Büchner shows little interest in the ravings of a madman; what obviously intrigues him is the nature of madness. By means of his multi-leveled structure he attempts to show that insanity is not the moving force, but the effect of Lenz's condition. Rather than personal failings, the repeated mental crises are seen as relatively normal responses to the human condition. No less than Danton (or perhaps any other man), Lenz is confronted by a chaotic mesh of seemingly divergent "realities." But whereas Danton admits to the impossibility of distinguishing what is real and what is illusion, Lenz, a far more fragile and perhaps more widely representative spirit, tries to cling to those beliefs which he considers essential to his survival.

Perhaps the most fundamental stabilizing force in Lenz is his faith in God and love for the nature He created. Not only does his religious belief form the basis of his concepts of nature and art, but in his anguish he turns to it for comfort; reciting prayers or reading from the Bible. Yet he cannot still the doubts which come over him at crucial moments. He envies Oberlin and the people of the village for the simplicity and fervor of their faith, but his psychological complexity will not allow him to emulate their simple devotion no matter how hard he tries. He finds himself fascinated by various mystical experiences as related to him by Oberlin and others. They tend to reinforce his faith, but the failure of all his efforts to receive a personal sign from God feeds his doubts again and again. Upon the death of Friederike, a young girl in a neighboring village, he reacts with violent fury:

He felt that he could raise a monstrous fist to the Heavens and tear God down and drag Him through His clouds; as if he could grind the world together with his teeth and spit it out into the Creator's face. . . . Lenz laughed loudly and with that laugh atheism took hold of him surely and calmly and firmly. . . . Everything was empty and hollow. . . .
The following day he awoke horrified by his state on the previous day. He stood now at an abyss, and derived a mad delight from looking down into it and reliving his torment. Then his terror increased; he was faced with his sin against the Holy Ghost.[20]

The cruelty of God's seeming indifference to human suffering is unbearable to Lenz. Yet atheism, the intellectual alternative, shakes the very foundation of his being. He is trapped in an irresolvable conflict. Facing the void of a Godless world is as impossible for him as is blind faith in a God who is capable of inflicting pain and suffering upon His creatures.

It is the desperation of this conflict which casts the darkest shadow over Lenz's life. His surroundings take on the appearance of the unreal. If there is no creator, how can there be a creation? This question, though it is not expressed in the text, always seems to hover over Lenz's most terrifying crises. The world seems to dissolve into a substanceless dream. The words *dream* and *dreamlike* appear with astonishing frequency to describe Lenz's perceptions, as, for example, in the following passage:

As his surroundings grew darker in shadow, everything seemed dreamlike to him, repugnant; anxiety took hold of him like a child who must sleep in the dark; he felt as if he were blind. And now it grew, this mountain of madness shot up at his feet; the hopeless thought that everything was a dream spread itself out in front of him; he clung to all solid objects. Figures rapidly passed him by, he pressed toward them, they were shadows, life withdrew from him, his limbs were numb.[21]

Such crises, and this is only one of several, reveal Lenz's proximity to a nihilism dangerously close to Danton's. They imply an almost complete breakdown of faith—not only in a religious sense, but also in an existential sense. No less than Danton, Lenz shows himself to be completely dependent upon his senses. When they falter, as in the above passage where darkness erases his vision, his spiritual equilibrium collapses, the whole structure of his existence crumbles away, life itself wanes.

In contrast to Danton, who coolly rejects all dogma, Lenz is stimulated all the more by the severity of his doubt. As soon as he comes to his senses, he devotes all his energies to the restoration of the threatened superstructure. With fervor he throws himself into various acts of penitence, helps Oberlin with parish duties, prepares a sermon for the Sunday services, and visits the sick in the hope of allaying their suffering. But when his senses again become impeded, when darkness descends or when mists shroud the landscape, the superstructure begins to collapse anew, and the cycle begins again. Fear turns to panic, he feels himself slipping into a dream world, then come feverish, instinctive attempts to stimulate the senses (scratching himself, pounding his head against the ground, throwing himself into cold water, etc.), followed by penitence and a relatively peaceful period often dominated by religious fervor and the desire to help others.

Mainly due to the unique structure of *Lenz*, which allows the reader an objective view of the hero's inner life without losing

sight of the outer world, a remarkable inversion of values is produced. If Lenz's actions were seen purely from the outside they
would certainly appear as inexplicable ravings of a madman.
While they might engender compassion for the sufferer, the reader
would not feel personally addressed by the work. Much the same
would be true if the story were told from the point of view of
Lenz himself. The reader would be in a position to reject all
association between Lenz's condition and his own, for he would
be led to feel that the work represented the twisted conceptions
of a diseased mind.

As it is, however, the reader cannot disassociate himself from
Lenz's fate quite so readily. It is evident that Lenz's frenzied
outbursts do not result from imaginary or even irrational fears.
On the contrary, the fears are well founded in the human condition as Büchner sees it. They stem from questions which the
mind is not equipped to resolve, questions which cast a shadow
over all human endeavors. On the other hand, faith, whether it
is in God, or in a universal order, or even faith in a world which
lies beyond immediate perceptions, no matter how essential for
survival, can be recognized as irrational response. In a moment of
reflection Lenz himself gives expression to the idea that man
actually invents his reality:

"Oh, this boredom! I scarcely know anymore what to say; I've drawn
all kinds of figures on the walls." Oberlin told him to turn to God; this
made Lenz laugh and say: "How I wish I were as fortunate as you
to have so comfortable a pastime. One could very easily spend his
time that way. Everything for idleness' sake. After all, most people
pray out of boredom, others fall in love out of boredom, some are
virtuous, some vicious, and I am nothing, absolutely nothing! I don't
even want to take my own life: it would be too boring!"[22]

Since the idea that all of man's actions result from his dread of
boredom reappears almost verbatim in *Leonce and Lena,* it obviously embodies one of Büchner's central conceptions.[23]

The clear and tragic implication is that man has invented an
arbitrary *raison d'être* to give substance to his strivings. As long
as he is unaware of the artificiality of this superstructure he can
function "normally" in society. However, rational inquiry into the
superstructure exposes the individual to great dangers. As in the
case of Danton, he could suffer a total disenchantment and with-

draw into a paralyzing cocoon of nihilism, or like Lenz he might panic at the sight of the dizzying abyss (a frequent Büchner symbol for the emptiness experienced by the nihilist) and become locked in a hopeless, often grotesque, struggle to buttress an undermined faith. The disquieting implication is that the whole question of sanity is a nebulous one indeed. Given the mind's limited capacity to recognize reality, who is more in tune with the real human condition, the so-called well-adjusted man who makes little effort to differentiate between reality and illusion, or the man whose mind cracks under the weight of doubts?

CHAPTER 4

Leonce and Lena[1]
Over the Edge

IT can hardly escape notice that the narrative perspective in *Lenz*, which is so constructed as to allow the reader to sense simultaneously the various layers of inner and outer reality, is essentially the perspective of the drama. The theater audience is quite naturally confronted with a juxtaposition of outer and inner reality. Stage setting, plot, and action establish reality at the outer level, while the dialogue gives insight into the inner world of the characters. Ironically, *Lenz* can therefore be taken as prime evidence for Büchner's strong inclination away from narrative and toward dramatic literature. Indeed, Büchner himself expressed his preference clearly when he wrote to his family on January 1, 1836: "I am sticking to the field of drama." While this statement might be taken as an indication of some uneasiness about his *Lenz,* which must have been in progress just at that time, it also implies considerable optimism about his future as a dramatist.

The announcement of a comedy writing contest by the book publisher Cotta on February 3, 1836, gave Büchner the impetus to start on a new project for the theater, *Leonce and Lena.* Since Büchner was not a fast writer, he overshot both the initially established and the extended deadline (August) set by the publisher. His finished manuscript was therefore returned to him unopened and unfortunately lost along with so many of his personal papers.[2] As several imperfections in the text show, the printed version relies on unpolished drafts which were first assembled for publication by Gutzkow in 1838.

Generally speaking, criticism of *Leonce and Lena* has involved tracing a multitude of ideas and themes which Büchner borrowed from previous writers. Some of the critics, such as Viëtor, Knight, or Lindenberger, show how the patchwork of Shakespeare

Leonce and Lena

and Brentano, Alfieri and Musset, Nestroy and Tieck develops into a quilt which bears the unique characteristics of Büchner's own genius. Others, Gundolf for example, dismiss the comedy as an unfortunate failure.[3] Masterwork or failure, the work is by no means easily put aside. Without a doubt, it offers the reader and the audience, as well as the critic, an even greater challenge than Büchner's other works. In it, all the common, time-tested ingredients of traditional comedy are carefully mixed together in such abundance as to form an altogether unorthodox, if not unique, work of art.

There can be little doubt that Shakespeare's *As You Like It*, from which Büchner takes his motto for the first act, is one of the most important sources for *Leonce and Lena*. The plots are quite closely related, and it would not be difficult to find parallels to all of Büchner's characters in this and other Shakespearean comedies. Yet, even a casual attempt at a comparison leads to the discovery that the two plays are of a totally different nature. Like most situation comedies, *As You Like It* depends on a plot of great intricacy and complexity. The dukes, the ladies and gentlemen of the court, the jesters, the fools, the lovesick shepherds, the man-chasing country lasses, and the rustic philosophers all run headlong through a maze of fantasy toward the quadruple wedding ceremony which brings the play to a happy conclusion. In direct contrast, Büchner's work is marked throughout by its stark economy and simplicity, by the same nakedness which characterizes all his writings.

The plot can be told in a few words, because it follows the deeply rutted tracks of a fairy tale familiar to all. A prince who does not wish to marry according to his father's choice leaves his homeland before he sees his intended bride. She also flees from the marriage, and "naturally" (though it is the most unnatural thing in the world) the two quickly find each other and fall in love. Before they become aware of each other's true identity, they are married and on the way to a happy-ever-after.

Innumerable dramas, both comedies and tragedies, are based on variations of this pattern. Generally, however, the obstacles encountered along the way give the material its dramatic substance. One or both of the partners love the wrong parties, or, perhaps, the attempt to escape an undesired marriage involves actions which make a reconciliation difficult or impossible. Perhaps a conflict between genuine love and admiration or gratitude in the manner of Rousseau's *Nouvelle Héloïse,* a version particularly common in the German theater of the late eighteenth and early nineteenth centuries, interferes with the smooth progression of the pattern; or, as in the case of Heinrich von Kleist's *Käthchen von Heilbronn,* facts about the background of one of the partners, which are seemingly crucial to the outcome of the drama, are withheld until the very end. The number of possibilities appears to be practically unlimited. Yet, without some sort of complication, without limitations or barriers (whether material, human, social, or moral) against which the lovers must struggle, the fairy tale is devoid of real dramatic effect. In *Leonce and Lena,* however, there is hardly a hint of any external obstacle. To be sure, there seems to be a conflict between father and son. King Peter decrees that his son is to marry the princess from a neighboring kingdom. Leonce rebels at the idea, but the ease with which he escapes his obligations by simply walking away from them shows that the King's power to impose his will is practically nonexistent. Leonce's rebellion seems to require no sacrifice and a minimum of inconvenience. Certainly the conflict could not be called dramatic. At no time is the audience led to fear the consequence of the action.

In fact, Büchner makes every effort to undermine the dramatic tension which traditionally attaches itself to this general theme. His lack of deviation from what might be called the raw conception of the fairy tale seems to be purposefully calculated to create an undramatic effect. It is true that a sophisticated audience, long used to conflicts brought about by a great variety of obstacles, might be held in a state of suspense merely by the fact that it expects *the problem* to arise at any moment. Such a twist, if successfully applied so that the audience itself becomes the butt of the joke, could be a good theatrical trick, but it would hardly constitute drama worthy of serious discussion. *Leonce and Lena* could scarcely be dismissed on the basis of trickery of this type.

Nevertheless, Büchner's resorting to an outworn plot in its most undramatic form creates a nagging problem. If *Leonce and Lena* is taken to be a romantic comedy in the style of Brentano or Arnim, as Gutzkow saw it,[4] and as Gundolf still saw it after it had finally reached the stage ninety years later, the problem largely dissolves, for the play then can be simply marked as a failure. Some astonishment might remain as to why, if he really wanted to write a comedy in accord with the romantic mode of his day for the sake of the contest in which it was to be entered, Büchner could not develop a more sophisticated plot. The extent of the failure of *Leonce and Lena* as a modish, romantic comedy can easily be measured by the fact that it was not considered stageworthy until long after the popular works of this genre had dropped out of sight, and the Büchner renaissance was well under way.

However, the idea that Büchner had in mind a romantic comedy when he wrote *Leonce and Lena* is not easily acceptable. No one, including Gutzkow, feels comfortable with it, especially when Büchner's impassioned argument against the falsification of reality is remembered, an argument which appears not only in *Lenz*, but also in a letter to his parents. His demand is for literary figures of "flesh and blood" rather than "marionettes with noses blue as the sky and with artificial pathos."[5] It seems hardly likely that Büchner suddenly overturned this most basic of his esthetic conceptions, particularly in view of the fact that the black images of *Woyzeck* must have taken shape in his mind even while he was working on his comedy. All external evidence points away from the conclusion that Büchner wanted to enter into competition with the fashionable writers of romantic farce on their own terms. There is hardly another poet in the first half of the nineteenth century who shows less affinity to romantic dreams. In *Danton* and *Lenz*, and later in *Woyzeck*, he shows himself to be a cynic who constructs sentimental images primarily for the purpose of smashing them. He does sometimes make use of devices traditionally associated with the romanticists. Thus songs in the pattern of familiar folk tunes appear in all his works, but the substance of these songs is in every case antiromantic. Their purpose is to annihilate the romantic dreams so dear to the heart of the previous generation and thereby to expose the raw tragedy of reality.

The fairy tale told by an old woman at the climax of *Woyzeck* is perhaps the most obvious example of this type of iconoclasm. Following the tradition-bound pattern of the *Volksmärchen*, it inverts the latter's purpose:

Once upon a time there was a poor little girl who had no father and no mother. Everyone was dead, and there was no one left in the whole wide world. Everyone was dead. And the little girl went out and looked for someone night and day. And because there was no one left on earth, she wanted to go to Heaven. And the moon looked down so friendly at her. And when she finally got to the moon, it was a piece of rotten wood. And so she went to the sun, and it was a faded sunflower. And when she got to the stars, they were little golden flies, stuck up there as if they were caught in a spider's web. And when she wanted to go back to earth, the earth was an upside-down pot. And she was all alone. And she sat down there and cried. And she sits there to this day, all, all alone.[6]

Instead of reaching for a piece of rotten wood and finding the moon, Büchner's little innocent heroine reaches for the moon and finds a rotten piece of wood. Instead of finding salvation by entering into a world of magic, as demanded by tradition, she faces one disillusionment after another, until nothing is left but unending and terrifying hopelessness. Instead of the transformation of an all too painful reality into a world of fantasy, Büchner shows the total collapse of the world of dreams under the stress of crises. His position would seem to be categorically antiromantic, and the use of typically romantic forms only serves to underscore his message: the attempt to lend meaning to human existence by building it upon a supernatural structure is nothing but a cruel hoax.

As has been previously shown, both *Danton* and *Lenz* contain similar, nihilistic messages. It is, therefore, difficult to accept *Leonce and Lena* simply as a flight of fancy, "gently mournful, cleverly jesting, with the ending brightened by the love of life for the sake of love," as Viëtor describes it.[7] While there is little justification in demanding consistency or even compatibility of ideas in different works by the same author, such apparently radical dichotomies do call for a search for alternative interpretations which might account for, or even heal, the breach.

Is it not possible that, in writing *Leonce and Lena*, Büchner had in mind an effect similar to that of the fairy tale cited above? On the surface, of course, there is little basis for a comparison. Not only does the comedy have a happy ending, but, as has been noted before, all signs of conflict are subdued. In fact, Leonce seems to have little trouble entering into a dream world where, all year long, "we shall . . . live amidst roses and violets, surrounded by orange and laurel boughs."[8] It seems that, for Leonce, the rotten piece of wood of the fairy tale has indeed turned into a moon which promises not only salvation but even perpetual bliss. But the very fact that the world suddenly dissolves into what is obviously a pipe dream distinctly limits the self-association of the audience with the hero. As one critic has pointed out in discussing the ending of the play, an ironic questioning of the conventions which make the happy ending possible is unavoidable.[9] Just as in the little tale about the forsaken child, the audience is brought face to face with the tragic contrast between dream and reality.

Unlike the fairy tale, which actually means to expose the cruelty inherent in false dreams, the ending of *Leonce and Lena* might still be linked to a device typical of the romanticists, namely romantic irony, which has precisely the aim of allowing the contrast between illusion and reality to become discernible. However, Büchner's use of this device is not governed by the same love of the dream world which guided the romanticists. A careful reading of the play reveals that the never-never land which opens before Leonce and Lena at the end is not a symbol of human ideals, but a symptom of the failure of the human mind.

The striking simplicity of the plot has the effect of throwing maximum attention upon the characters, for while the plot lacks tension, there is no lack of surprise in the personalities who appear on the stage. Perhaps most unexpected, and definitely most important, is the character of the hero, Prince Leonce. It is immediately obvious that he is anything but the shining knight whose role he plays in the myth which shapes the plot. Right from the beginning, his character is portrayed with a depth usually reserved for tragic heroes; indeed, his brooding in the first act brings to mind a Hamlet or a Romeo more than an Orlando, his approximate counterpart in *As You Like It*. Although his opening remarks have a comic ring, they gradually betray deep suffering:

. . . Do you see this stone? My first duty is to spit down upon it three-hundred-and-sixty-five times in succession. . . . And then do you see this handful of sand? . . . I throw it into the air. Shall we wager? How many grains of sand have I now on the back of my hand? An odd or an even number? . . . And then I must ponder the possibilities of how I shall go about seeing the top of my head. Oh, for the man who shall see the top of his head for the first time! . . . And then an endless number of things of such sort. Am I an idler? Am I temporarily unoccupied? Yes, and isn't it sad . . . that the clouds have been drifting from west to east now for fully three weeks. It has made me terribly melancholy.[10]

What seems to start as a satirical exposure of idleness among the rich and privileged—still a favorite, though somewhat antiquated, comic theme in Büchner's day—begins to turn sour with the realization that Leonce is not just another version of the corrupt, mildly frustrated aristocrat, but a man suffering from an extremely dangerous malady. It is noteworthy that his introspection, not his action, exposes the uselessness of his existence. Therefore, his isolation from the world of action, his lack of real accomplishment and true mission in life, are seen in psychological, not sociological, terms. Leonce's feelings and thoughts, not his role in society, become the focal center and throw dark clouds over the comedy from the very beginning.

As the continuation of the opening passage makes clear, Leonce does not fail to recognize the disease which infects him:

. . . Indolence is the beginning of all evil. What people won't do out of mere boredom! They study out of boredom, pray out of boredom, they love, they marry and multiply out of boredom, and then at last they die out of boredom, and—what makes it so amusing—they do it with the most serious countenances, without ever understanding why, and God knows what all else. These heroes, these geniuses, these simpletons, these saints, these sinners, these fathers of families, are, after all, nothing more than refined indolent idlers. Why must *I* be the one to know this? Why can't I be important to myself . . . ?

Like so many other figures in Büchner's works, from *Danton* to *Woyzeck*, Leonce suffers severe disenchantment with human existence. The idea that everything in life is done out of boredom undermines all human knowledge and striving. Leonce's formulations are, of course, not without comic effect, but the humor is the sardonic product of a stricken mind, a mind which has all but thought itself out of existence by reaching the devastating conclusion that there is nothing to know, and that, therefore, all

endeavors are utterly meaningless gestures. Throwing sand in
the air is equated in importance with those aspects of life that
are commonly considered most vital to existence: love, and
propagation. Leonce's speculations go so far as to imply that the
brain is no more than an unfortunate trick of nature, a complicated mechanism which has a certain potential but no real function. It has pretensions to the power of knowing even though
there is nothing to know.
It is obvious that such conceptions have deeply tragic overtones. In fact, Leonce's nihilism can hardly be differentiated
from Danton's, and the similarity of his remarks to one of Lenz's
most anguished outbursts of hopelessness cannot escape notice;
the actual wording varies only slightly.[11] In order to make such
a shattering theme suitable for comic treatment, Büchner attempts to take the chain of ideas one step further than in either
of his previous works. The kind of mind which questions human
values to the point of actually casting doubt upon the functions
of the brain will inevitably reach the point where it can no longer
take itself seriously. It is perfectly logical that the nihilistic mind
should, in the end, lose faith in itself; but this type of logic is
pernicious and can only be associated with madness, for it
threatens the mind with self-inflicted extinction.
There are important hints in Leonce's opening statement that
he is tottering on the brink of precisely this kind of insanity. No
matter how true his nihilistic broodings might ring, they immediately characterize him as socially maladjusted in such a way that
he would generally be branded as suffering from serious mental
disorders. The question, so important in *Danton* and *Lenz,* as to
whether it is actually the alienated social misfit or the well-adjusted member of society whose sanity must be ultimately
doubted is of only secondary interest in *Leonce and Lena*, since
Büchner focuses all attention upon the insidiously self-defeating
aspects of Leonce's mind and excludes well-functioning members
of society from the cast altogether. The crucial symptom of
Leonce's mental crisis is revealed in his bitter outcry, "Why can't
I be important to myself?," clearly betraying a skepticism aimed
not only against the outside world but also against himself. Short
of a miracle, a man who cannot be important to himself, and
whose ego is destroyed because his mind rebels against itself,
would seem to be doomed to a tragic fate, indeed.

Yet can madness not be a kind of miraculous, if perverse, blessing? It has frequently been treated as such in literature. When suffering becomes unbearable, madness can offer an escape. Such an idea is expressed in *Danton* when Camille says, in reference to his beloved Lucille: "There was madness behind those eyes. She's not the first to go mad—that's what the world makes of us. . . . Heaven help her find a comfortable delusion. . . . The only way to be happy is to imagine yourself Father, Son, and Holy Ghost all in one."[12] What greater blessing is there for the tortured mind than complete escape from unbearable realities? This seems to be Camille's message here, and approximately the same idea rings forth from Büchner's motto for the first act of *Leonce and Lena,* a quotation from the words of Jacques, Shakespeare's bitter melancholiac in *As You Like It:* "Oh! that I were a fool, I am ambitious for a motley coat." The conception of madness as an escape from a cruel reality can only be understood as an outgrowth of the ultimate despair. It often becomes a haunting theme in tragedy, as for example in *Hamlet.* Ophelia's flight into madness, even though it relieves the grief of her last days, intensifies the tragedy. A personal victory over torment, madness nevertheless is seen as a tragedy in a universal sense. In comedy, the effect can be even more devastating. If the donning of a motley coat is seen as an escape into unrestrained bliss, as it can in the comedy, madness is elevated to the highest human aspiration, actually making a bitter mockery of man's endless, often unrewarding struggle for happiness. By implication, the very essence of human striving becomes senseless.

Büchner leaves little doubt as to the significance of his Shakespearean motto, for Jacques' lament is also Leonce's. It is apparent from the beginning that Leonce's life has become intolerably meaningless to him. There seems to be no way out of his morass of despair when he cries out: "My God, to be able to be someone else! For only a moment." Though he does not actually repeat Jacques' wish to be a "fool," the connection is immediately defined by the subsequent action. No sooner do the words pass over his lips when, a little like a *deus ex machina,* Valerio, "somewhat inebriated," skips onto the stage. "Look at the fool run!" Leonce shouts, and adds longingly: "I wish I knew of only one thing under the sun that still could make me run like that."

Valerio, whose free spirit Leonce would like to be able to

Leonce and Lena

emulate, is easily recognizable as a "fool" in the earthy tradition
of Touchstone, whose motley coat Jacques envies in *As You Like
It*. However, Büchner gives the concept "fool" a much more distinctly clinical meaning than Shakespeare, as Valerio's comments
on the subject show. In a passage which must be considered one
of the important keys to *Leonce and Lena*, Valerio responds to
Leonce's admonitions with a rather thorough definition:

LEONCE: Oh, keep quiet with your songs! They are enough to make
a man a fool.
VALERIO: At least he'd be *something*. A fool! What man would barter
his foolhood against my reason? Ha! I'm an Alexander the Great!
Look how the sun makes a golden crown of my hair, how my uniform
sparkles! Lord Generalissimo Grasshopper, let the troops advance!
Lord Chancellor of the Exchequer, bring me some money! My dear
Lady-in-Waiting Dragonfly, how is my precious spouse Madam Bean
Pole getting along? . . . And because of such exquisite fantasies as
these one receives good soup, good meat, good bread, a good bed,
and a gratuitous cutting of the hair—that is to say in the madhouse—
while I with my sound reason can, at best, do nothing more than take
a position as one who promotes the advancement of blossoms on cherry
trees. . . .[13]

"Foolhood" is thus distinctly associated with the madhouse. Perhaps reflecting the modernization of social institutions, Büchner's
"fool" no longer enjoys the freedom to roam the face of the earth
as a jester. He is allowed to engage his folly only within the narrow confines of the insane asylum. However, what the Shakespearean jester accomplished in private practice, the modern
"fool" achieves through socialization: he receives good food, a
good bed—in other words: a comfortable life with no other responsibility than allowing his fantasy to soar.

Through Valerio's words, Büchner establishes the madhouse
as the ultimate human goal. It is the closest approximation of the
land of milk and honey which the real world has to offer. It is
the place where all needs are cared for and nothing is expected
but those delicious dreams which cut away the pain of the outside world. As Valerio sees it, the madhouse is the only place on
earth which offers a life free from care, free from want, free of
serious conflict, and even free of the vast emptiness which throws
such a dark shadow over Leonce's existence. A man can become

Alexander the Great there and lead an exciting life among generals and courtiers without facing the consequences of real decisions.

Is there not a striking similarity between Valerio's conception of the madhouse and the world as it is portrayed and populated within the play as a whole? Even the names of the toy kingdoms where the action takes place, Pipi and Popo (the German equivalents of those important childhood terms *peepee* and *fanny*), sound like proclamations made from the throne in the privy by not overly profound founders. Saving perhaps Lena and Leonce, everyone from King to peasant is peculiarly unburdened by consequential problems. Despite the fact that they are uniquely unsuited for their various roles in the world, they seem well fed and well cared for. Not one eyebrow is raised at the mad antics which occupy all the inhabitants of the kingdom. No one from the President of the Council of State, who cannot stop snapping his fingers while speaking, to the schoolmaster, who decks out a group of peasants with branches of fir, so that they will look like a forest to the royal procession, injects even a trace of sanity into the realm. But the maddest figure of all is the King, whose love for philosophizing about his duties and his clothes while dressing leads to the most absurd nonsense:

Man was made to think, and still I must think for my subjects; because they cannot think for themselves. . . . The substance of the matter is considered in the abstract, and I am that abstract. [*He runs about the room half naked.*] Is that understood? To be considered in the abstract is to be considered in the abstract. Do you understand? And now my attributes come forward, my modifications, my affections and accidentals: where is my shirt, my trousers? Stop? Oh, shame! What do you mean leaving my free will here so exposed! What's happened to morality: where are my cuffs? . . .[14]

Such relatively lighthearted farce, of course, contains obvious elements of political satire. Yet the barbs are anything but sharpened. While King Peter is certainly totally inept, he also proves to be completely ineffective. His fumbling ineptitude is balanced by an equally evident lack of ambition. Other than the proclamation that his son is to marry the princess from the neighboring kingdom of Pipi, there is not the slightest sign of any oppressive scheme which would encourage the idea that Büchner seriously wanted to satirize the petty tyrants of his time. Indeed, by the time Peter, at the end of the drama, voluntarily abdicates his throne in favor of the prince so that he can devote himself, along with his staff of "wise philosophers," to "uninterrupted thought," it is clear that life in Popo has only the most incidental similarities to life in the world outside the walls of the madhouse.

The only figure in the play whose madness seems to betray a measure of duplicity is Valerio; for despite the fact that he is cast in the role of the arch-fool, he is the only one who, on occasion, sees through the veil of surrealism. Quite in keeping with his idealization of the madhouse, his antics seem to be calculated to keep him well fed. Yet, not only with his previously cited words, but throughout the drama, he speaks with a cynicism which betrays his awareness that all the furor around him is but a game of make-believe. Through the clouds of dreams, his is the only voice which injects a note of rational judgment. He therefore becomes a most important figure, for without him, all connection with the world of reality would disappear from the play.

When, at the end of the first scene, Leonce embraces him as one who "wanders effortlessly through the sweat and dust on the highway of life," Valerio becomes more than just a companion, he actually becomes a guide, in a sense, perhaps even a healer.

The hopelessness of alleviating the suffering of a man tottering on the brink of madness by attempting to steer him back to "normalcy" is explored in Lenz. Leonce and Lena (the names sound like somewhat comic echoes of Lenz) seems to be an examination of the only alternative. That this alternative can only be understood as an expression of scathing cynicism is self-evident. Instead of trying to hold a man back and keep him from falling over the brink, give him a gentle push! Precisely this seems to be the task which Valerio assigns to himself. Unlike Oberlin, who patiently tries to coach Lenz back to reason, Valerio greets each symptom of Leonce's degenerating mental state with applause. Indeed, by the third scene he is already able to determine that Leonce "seems to be on the best of all possible ways to becoming a veritable fool."[15]

These words of "hope" come in response to one of Leonce's mournful monologues which is overheard by Valerio, hiding under the table. The agony of total alienation which rings forth in this monologue is a distinct echo of both Danton and Lenz.

Recalling the motif of the mosaic Venus de'Medici which Danton seeks piecemeal among the Parisian whores,[16] Leonce's desperation is brought to a climax when he realizes that his sexuality offers no sanctuary from his estrangement: "My God, how many women we need to be able to sing the scale of love up and down again! One is scarcely enough to provide a single tone. Why must this haze over our earth be a prism to break down love's white ray of passion into a rainbow?"[17] His lingering belief in the healing power of love finally shattered, Leonce finds himself on the verge of a Lenzlike collapse. He feels trapped in a vacuum without any hope of escape. Not even intoxicants hold out the promise of mellowing the pain of existence:

[*He drinks*] In what bottle is the wine hiding that's to make me drunk today? Or won't I ever get that far! I feel as if I were sitting under an air pump. The air is so rare it makes me freeze . . .—Come Leonce, let's have a monologue, I want to listen. —My life gapes at me like a vast expanse of white paper which I'm to fill, but I can't produce so much as a single letter. My head is an empty ballroom: some wilted flowers and crumbled ribbons on the floor, cracked violins in the corner, the last dancers have taken off their masks and look at one another with eyes tired as death. Twenty-four times a day I turn myself inside out like a glove . . . —Bravo Leonce! Bravo! [*He applauds*] It does me good to cheer myself that way. . . .

Leonce displays a virtual parade of symptoms all of which point to imminent mental collapse. He sees life as a vast emptiness within which he is incapable of functioning. Flowers, ribbons, and violins, commonplace symbols for festive gaiety, turn into symbols of futility and sham. The deathly weariness in the eyes of the unmasked dancers represents the dreary actuality which confronts Leonce, subverting the memory of the dream which once seemed so real. For Leonce, the dreamlike masquerade has ended, and the reality he faces leaves little room for hope. Leonce sees his future as a meaningless, endlessly monotonous state of boredom.

Yet it is precisely at this moment that Valerio expresses his cheerful assessment of the situation. The fact that Leonce finds within himself the urge to scoff at his own tragic conceptions undoubtedly offers the best reason for his optimism. When Leonce mockingly applauds his own debilitating inspirations he demonstrates his inner rebellion in the clearest possible terms. He shows that he can no longer take his own ideas seriously. In effect, his mind begins to attack its own thoughts. To Valerio this self-destructive mental process is an encouraging sign, for it is clear to him that Leonce's only remaining hope lies in the severing of all connections with the problems of reality. If he is to find happiness in the magic make-believe world surrounding him, Leonce must erase from his mind the painful memories of that world outside the walls where existence is so problematical.

Still within the same scene, in response to Leonce's plea that Valerio help him out of his dilemma, Valerio, by a series of suggestions, attempts to persuade him that his problems actually have little relevance to the circumstances in which he finds himself. In what appears to be a direct response to Leonce's previously cited wish "to be someone else," if only for a moment, Valerio's recommendations clearly imply that all the barriers in the way of a new identity are self-imposed. If being Prince Leonce has become an unbearable burden, then, according to Valerio, "We shall become learned gentlemen . . . let's become heroes . . . we'll become geniuses . . . why don't we just simply go to hell!"[18] Surely this kind of advice is meant to convince Leonce (and the audience) that freedom in the kingdom of Popo is limited only by the imagination. Any dream, no matter how fanciful, can assume the proportions of a new reality, provided only that the mental remnants of an earlier life can be extinguished.

Forgetting is the key to the magic world of the madhouse. Even with the supposition that the entire action of the play takes place within the confines of an insane asylum, there can be no question but that Leonce's suffering is caused by his insights into the disharmony of the real world. As Valerio's numerous comments show, Leonce, at the beginning of the second act, is not yet a full-fledged "fool." It is not until the end of the second scene of Act II that he earns that title.[19] Until that moment he is described as still being "on the way" to the madhouse. The madhouse, then, is not only a physical, but also, and foremost, a mental state, which can only be entered through an exit—both physical and mental—from the outside world. Büchner does not throw much light on the precise psychological process of finding such an exit. Since the idealization of the madhouse, as stated before, can only be understood as an expression of bitter cynicism, self-imposed brainwashing techniques lie quite outside the scope of the play. Nevertheless, Büchner hints at forces akin to the "obscure instinct" which is repeatedly invoked to explain Lenz's capacity for survival.[20] Leonce's memory is apparently extinguished by a no less mysterious and opportune "inner voice," as indicated by the motto to the second act, consisting of the following lines from the poem "Die Blinde" ("The Blind Woman") by Adelbert von Chamisso:

> But yet a voice began to sound
> From deep within me
> And in a single moment drowned
> All my memory.[21]

There is little basis for speculation about the nature of this inner voice. It must simply be regarded as a kind of deus ex machina both invisible and inaudible to the audience. On the surface, the second act deals with Leonce's flight (which in one afternoon, according to Valerio's accounting, leads through "a dozen principalities, through half a dozen grand duchies and through several kingdoms")[22] and his meeting with Lena, who, though only sketchily characterized in the last scene of the first act, clearly suffers from precisely the same spiritual deprivation as the prince himself. There can be no question that Lena is the external stimulus for the turnabout which eventually makes the dark images that had haunted Leonce disappear. In a way, Leonce's salvation can be properly ascribed to the triumph of love. Yet Büchner does everything in his power to undermine the elation which would normally attach itself to such a theme, thereby minimizing the importance of love as a genuinely healing force.

The dark, often bitter tone of the first act continues throughout the second. To a large extent, this tone can be attributed to the harsh, often cruel imagery which saturates even the most tender exchanges. In fact, the most strikingly despondent images come with Leonce's declaration of love:

LENA [to herself]: . . . The moon is like a slumbering child . . . its sleep is death. Like a lifeless angel lying on a dark cushion, and the stars, like candles, burning round about him! How sad it is, to be dead and so alone.

LEONCE: Rise up then in your moon-white dress and wander through the night behind its lifeless form and sing a song of death!

LENA: Who's there?

LEONCE: A dream.

LENA: Dreams, they say, are blest.

LEONCE: Then dream yourself blest and let me be your blessèd dream.

LENA: Death is the most blessèd dream.

LEONCE: Then let me be your Angel of Death! Let my lips, like his wings, light upon your eyes. [*He kisses her*] Lovely, lifeless form, you rest so sweetly upon the pall of night that Nature, grown tired of living, is enamored of death.[23]

The association of love with death forms a fairly consistent motif in Büchner's works, yet nowhere is the effect more shocking than in this passage. Not vitality and hope, but a deep, unyielding, desperate sadness sounds forth as the images unfold. Love is seen not as a healing force which binds the wounds of life, but, on the contrary, as a power which unites the spirit with death. It is their common wish for death which forms the bonds of love between Leonce and Lena. In some ways, the association between love and death echoes a favorite romantic motif that is particularly dominant in the works of Novalis (1772–1801); but here, as always, Büchner inverts the purpose. While Leonce shares the romanticists' often expressed weariness of life, and even their "Yearning for Death" (the title of a Novalis hymn),[24] there is no trace of the trancelike timelessness of the afterlife which reunites all lovers in a spiritual existence free of the fetters of life on earth. Instead, the idea of death fills Lena with a strikingly mild emotion; she feels "sad" about it, for, as she sees it, to be dead is to be alone. That death, nevertheless, "is the most blessed dream," can only mean that even eternal solitude, sad as it is, represents the highest conceivable bliss. In effect, Büchner deromanticizes (or neutralizes) death, which emerges as neither a fearful nor a hopeful image but rather as a slightly preferable and, at the same time, hardly inspiring alternative to life. Leonce, as the Angel of Death, is not guided by a dream of a spiritual union with Lena in a world beyond, but rather by a vision of her "lifeless form"—a considerably softened translation of Büchner's harsh, unromantic term *Leiche* (corpse).

Despite its gloominess, Leonce's vision of Lena as a beautiful corpse inspires an immediate change in him. "All my being existed in that single moment! I wish I could die!" he shouts. "How fresh and clean all things seem to me now as they wrest their way from chaos." Certainly, this single moment of elation must be equated with the single moment which, according to Büchner's motto, drowns out all memory. Even though Leonce's first impulse is suicidal (Valerio must save him "from the most beautiful suicide I'll ever find"), a new world suddenly emerges from the chaos. "The earth is a golden bowl sparkling with light," he notes, and the light seems to dazzle him as it blots out all the sinister visions of reality.

Büchner makes no attempt to make Leonce's sudden rebirth at the end of the second act rationally convincing. The process is shown simply as a sudden miracle, and Leonce, when he returns in the last act, is a totally transformed individual. But this transformation hardly implies a rejection of the validity of Leonce's former conceptions by the author. Had it really been Büchner's intention to show the power of love in rehabilitating the totally alienated nihilist, then surely this process would have demanded explication. Indeed, the progress of the rehabilitation would properly be the focal center of the entire play. A step-by-step rejection of the nihilistic arguments which are so convincingly presented in the earlier scenes might properly be expected. Yet Büchner, except for the brief, and by no means completely enlightening, passage cited above, skips over Leonce's courtship of Lena, which, though short in time (the two are blissfully married less than a day after their meeting), is nevertheless decisive in effect. The stressed suddenness of the transformation underscores the point that love does not actually rehabilitate the prince at all. On the contrary, love awakens the seemingly instinctive "inner voice" which blots out whatever remains of Leonce's connection with reality. In other words, his salvation at the same time means the destruction of his "healthy" intellect. No longer capable of clear thought, he is also spared the suffering which had made his previous life a torturous nightmare.

As Valerio, who introduces the disguised lovers to the assembled wedding party in the final scene of the play, explains it, the two, in their present state, are not genuine human beings, but rather "automatons . . . of either sex . . . so consummately constructed that they cannot be differentiated from other human beings."[25] While Valerio's prime concern in speaking these words is keeping the identity of the two fugitives hidden, his description of them as automatons certainly must be understood as a symbolic reference to their loss of memory and intellect. Mechanically, they still function perfectly, but they have lost the power of critical thought. Therein lies their salvation and the ironic foundation of the "happy" ending of the play.

As in Büchner's previous works, happiness and intellectual fervor are placed at opposite poles. The individual who devotes himself uncompromisingly to the search for truth comes face to face with the perilous realization that illusion and reality cannot be differentiated by the mind. The more incisive the mind, the greater the uncertainty. Uncertainty leads to ever more fundamental questioning, ever more desperate searching, and ever increasing doubt. Danton, fully aware of this fact, accepts this tragic, descending spiral as human fate, does little to break away from it, and is ultimately destroyed by it. Lenz, again and again confronted by momentary visions of this spiral, shies away from them by attempting to recapture a childlike faith in God and nature; but, incapable of holding such simple beliefs because of his overly incisive intellect, he cannot escape the descent into ever increasing pathos. Leonce, however, does manage to escape the treacherous spiral when his intellect is more or less magically destroyed, enabling him, once again, to see the world through the gullible eyes of a child who does not distinguish between fairy tale and reality.

Precisely this task of distinction is given heavy emphasis in Leonce's very last speech. Having just accepted the reins of power from his father's hands, the prince ponders the problem of what is to be done with the realm in the following terms: "And so, Lena, you see how our pockets are stuffed with puppets and playthings. What shall we do with them? Shall we make mustaches for them and hang broadswords about their waists? Or shall we dress them in frock coats and let them practice infusorial politics and diplomacy, and sit here watching them through our microscopes?"[26] The subjects and possessions are called "puppets and playthings" by the new ruler. There is obvious political satire inherent in this formulation; but, beyond that, the passage again brings to focus the question of the relationship between reality and fancy. Does Leonce look upon real subjects and a real country as puppets and toys, or does he look upon a make-believe world surrounding him as reality? Are the puppets real people, or are they perhaps real puppets? Actually, they seem to be Leonce's fellow inmates. But no matter what is real and what is imagined, it is clear that, in the end, Leonce sees the world in the simple terms of a child playing in the nursery. His intellect, which only a day earlier had driven him to suicidal desperation, is gone, and he lives a blissfully simple existence as if he were living in a fairy tale.

Among the many more or less significant literary sources for *Leonce and Lena,* there is one from which Büchner might well have drawn certain motifs closely related to his central theme. While there is, of course, a far-reaching transformation in the form of expression, Goethe's *Werther* contains a short passage embodying much of the essence of *Leonce and Lena.* One of the crucial determinants of Werther's final plunge into suicide is a chance confrontation with a former inmate of an insane asylum. On November 30, less than a month before his death, he encounters this man, Heinrich, looking for flowers along a wintry river's edge. The scene itself seems to foreshadow Valerio's comment about Leonce's progress toward foolhood: "I can see him now . . . on an ice-cold, winter day . . . as he stands in the long shadows of bare trees, fanning himself with his handkerchief."[27] In both cases, the division between inner and outer reality is demonstrated by a basic environmental disorientation. Winter and summer are confused. But the most striking relationship here is the makeup of the inner world. Heinrich, too, lives in a world of kings and emperors. He, too, is in love with a princess. As Werther learns by questioning the young man's mother, he, too, had found happiness "in the madhouse, when he didn't know what was going on around him."[28] Werther's response to this confrontation not unexpectedly turns to mournful introspection: "Oh dear God in heaven, hast Thou made it man's fate that he cannot be happy until he has found his reason and lost it again? Poor wretch! Yet how I envy him pining away in his confusion. He goes out hopefully in the winter to pick flowers for his queen . . . and I? I go out without hope in my heart, with no purpose, and return home as I went."[29] Werther's envy of the "poor wretch," whose childish hopefulness stands in stark contrast to his own inner void, certainly cuts close to the center of Büchner's thinking in *Leonce and Lena*. More immediately pertinent than similarities between the motif in Goethe's novel and the main theme in Büchner's play is the strikingly different effect. Despite Werther's envy, Heinrich is indeed a poor wretch. He arouses the kind of sentiment—a sort of sad hopelessness—which attaches itself automatically to the harmlessly insane, no matter whether they are suffering or joyous. The sympathy for Leonce, on the other hand, is based upon his particular emotional state. His problems seem real, and there is a genuine feeling of relief when his suffering suddenly gives way to childish bliss. To be sure, the social implications of the play coincide perfectly with Werther's outcry, ". . . hast Thou made it man's fate that he cannot be happy until he has found his reason and lost it again?" To be sure, the idea that madness offers the only escape from an unbearable existence is a tragic one. Yet, Büchner involves the audience so deeply in Leonce's personal problems that the effect of the happy ending is actually elating, even though the elation is steeped in bitter irony.

Perhaps in order to avoid the danger of making his hero into a "poor wretch" who can be pitied but not loved, that is, in order to establish real empathy for him, Büchner does not put the label of the madman upon him. Instead, he makes him into a prince, that is, he presents him in Leonce's own—sometimes terrifying and sometimes comically twisted—world. Except for Valerio's occasional hints, there is no background of sanity against which the insanity can be contrasted. Despite Valerio's vision, Leonce is not actually seen in shirtsleeves on the stage fanning himself with a handkerchief in the dead of winter. Instead, he stands against the background of a make-believe royal palace, where his words and actions hardly seem odd in comparison with the peculiarities of those around him.

By approaching the theme of madness, so to speak, from within, Büchner mitigates the alienating effects of a madman's words and gestures. However, such an approach has the possible disadvantage of making insanity seem too comprehensible and, hence, sane. Seen from within, madness can hardly be expected to look altogether insane. Büchner seems to have created the

somewhat ambiguous figure of Valerio, the sane fool, to over-
come precisely this problem, but, judging by the general critical
reception of the play, his attempt was perhaps less than completely successful.

CHAPTER 5

Woyzeck

The Enemy Within

THE story of a simple soldier who murders his girl in a fit of jealous rage becomes the theme of a tragedy which Büchner wrote during the last months of his life. The play comes to us as a fragment without a real ending.[1] It nevertheless has become Büchner's most acclaimed and most frequently performed work. There is something almost uncanny about the spell it casts over audiences. Extraordinarily short, it vibrates with its compact intensity. A good performance need last no longer than forty minutes, although there are almost thirty scenes. The new dramatic structure, first attempted in *Danton,* is here brought to perfection. The division into acts disappears and so does character development. Plot is kept to a minimum. Just a series of stark pictures, brief confrontations between a humble man and the various people who populate his narrow world: his boss, his girl, a comrade, his child, his rival. The action skips from place to place. The Inn, Marie's Room, The Town, At the Doctor's, On the Street, At the Pond—these are the names of the scenes, and they designate the places that make up the daily world of every plain, ordinary man.

It is especially the structure of the play which strikes us today as radical, but in 1837, when Büchner planned to publish it, the theme would have been just as startling. Here is a proletarian tragedy, some eight years before the modern bourgeois tragedy had been made respectable with the appearance of Friedrich Hebbel's *Maria Magdalene!* Even more shocking: kindly sympathy for a man who viciously murders a woman right on the stage! And it is not just any murderer, for Woyzeck is not the perverse invention of a writer, but an extraordinarily faithful portrait of one of the most publicized killers of the time. Actually, more than a dozen years had passed since the criminal had been executed, but the controversy over the case was still smoldering. Questions about the legal accountability of the culprit continued to be debated. One side was, in effect, saying that the murderer had most certainly been a psychopath, and for that reason his life should have been spared. The other side, defending the execution, and supported by the official findings of an examining physician, claimed that there had been no convincing indications of insanity in the man, and that, in any case, he had shown no undue signs of a loss of self-control just before, during, and after the crime. Passions were running high in the controversy because the legal concepts involved were still new and were felt by many to be dangerously radical. But looking at the situation from the point of view of either side, where was the basis for dramatic sympathy here? Is a homicidal madman a more sympathetic figure than a rational, but cold-blooded, murderer?

There has always been a tendency on the part of interpreters of *Woyzeck* to assume that the tragedy represents a strictly partisan alignment, on the part of Büchner, with those who attacked the use of the death penalty in this case. That the play was, in fact, Büchner's statement on the continuing controversy can hardly be disputed, and it can also be quite properly assumed that he would have stood on the liberal side of the issue, especially since the power to deal out the death penalty rested in the hands of the reactionaries throughout Germany. However, to shape the story of this particular murderer into an effective weapon in the fight against the injustices of criminal law enforcement, it would have been necessary to characterize him as indisputably insane in the legal sense of the word. But the very notion of legal insanity is antithetical to one of Büchner's most fundamental ideas, for it presupposes a distinction between rational and irrational behavior which Büchner had thematically and categorically rejected in every one of his previous literary works. Over and over again, he had made the point that it was the well-adjusted, so-called sane people who were motivated by irrational impulses. The power of reason had stood on the side of the maladjusted, lost souls like Danton and Lenz who, because of it, became aliens in a world that stood beyond comprehension. In such a world, stripped of all signs of rational order, the concept that a man is not accountable before the law because of his irrationality is absurd, for it is based on an assumption of rational normalcy which cannot be sustained.

To see that the world of *Woyzeck* is no more orderly than that of *Danton* requires only the most superficial reading. Indeed, the wordless language of the play's structure with its fractured scenes, each abrasively clashing with the next, arranged to develop contrasts rather than continuities, speaks distinctly enough, not of reason, but of chaos in the world. If Büchner, then, did not actually take a position in the battle lines of the controversy over the case, what was it that drew him to the story of this criminal, which, after all, was well known and did not need retelling? It had been sensationalized in the press and was a matter of public record. Could he have seen, in the agony of this wretched man, the ultimate expression of the same tragic principle which had destroyed the minds of his earlier heros? Danton, the political theorist, Lenz, the poet, and Leonce, the idle thinker, they all became the victims of an overly powerful and uncompromising intellect. They all came to that same terrifying conclusion which had driven Goethe's Faust into the arms of Mephistopheles: coming to know that there was nothing to know. But for them there was no romantic savior from the underworld. And poor Woyzeck, the part-time soldier, struggling only with the mundane realities of a simple existence, was not even he safe from this disease of the titans?

The history of the murder as Büchner found it goes something like this:[2] On June 21, 1821, Johann Woyzeck, a forty-one-year-old unemployed former soldier, one-time barber, occasional bookbinder's helper, now homeless, was aimlessly, perhaps angrily, walking the streets of Leipzig. At four o'clock in the afternoon, he was supposed to have had a rendezvous with a woman, the forty-six-year-old widow Woost, in a park, but she had not appeared. Once his relations with her had been very close; there had even been talk of marriage. Yet all the warmth had faded away of late. Woyzeck sensed that his increasing difficulties in getting even temporary, menial employment had made her contemptuous of him. She seemed to be ashamed of being seen with him. He knew that she was being unfaithful to him. One night he had stalked her to a dance hall, had seen her whirling in another man's arms, and overheard her say to him, "Don't stop, don't stop!" His jealousy had led to numerous wild scenes. Once he had pushed her down a flight of stairs, picked up a rock to strike her, but had hesitated and dropped it harmlessly on the ground. There had been other displays of anger marked by violence. But she still occasionally sought him out for sexual gratification in out-of-the-way places. Sometime during his wanderings that afternoon, Woyzeck stopped at a shop to get a new handle for a broken knife he had purchased a few days before. On that previous day he had heard an inner voice urging him, "Stab Woost dead." "You are not going to do that," his conscience had replied, but the voice had come back again. "Yes, you'll do it," it had insisted. Later on, when his path took him past a pond near one of the city gates, he felt a sudden urge to throw the knife into the water, but he didn't. At about dusk on this, the longest day of the year, he suddenly spotted Mrs. Woost on the street. At first, he was happy to see her but quickly noticed her uneasiness in his presence. He assumed that she was afraid her other lover might see them together. Partially to spite her, he then insisted on walking her home. They got to her place about 9:30 P.M. As they entered the door, he heard her say, "I don't know what it is you want from me! Get out of here! What'll happen if the landlord comes?" Her tone enraged him. Only now he thought of the knife again. Before he knew what he was doing he had already driven it deeply into her breast. He drew it back and thrust again and again, seven times in all. He felt a sudden sense of relief, like a weight lifted from his heart. He walked away quickly, no one tried to stop him; and as he passed one of the city squares, he momentarily thought of stabbing himself, too, but there were too many people around. He would do it later, he promised himself. But then the police were suddenly there to arrest him. He surreptitiously tried to dispose of the knife, but it was too late.

On the way to the police station, he asked if Mrs. Woost was dead. When nobody answered he said, "God let her be dead, she deserves it for what she did to me." At the interrogation that same night, it never occurred to him to deny anything. He made a full confession including the details indicated here. It agreed completely with the testimony of several witnesses. His answers to questions were cited for their responsiveness and lucidity in the records.

In view of the detailed confession, the trial at first seemed to be nothing but a formality. The public defender had already filed his routine defense summary, and the case was in the hands of the judge when rumors of periodic attacks of insanity in the defendant's life began to appear in the press. This moved the defense counselor to petition the court to reopen the case for the purpose of a psychiatric examination. In response to this petition, Dr. Johann Clarus, a clinical professor from the medical school of the University of Leipzig, held a series of five interview and examination sessions with the defendant. Two days after the last of these he reported his findings, namely, that he could uncover no evidence in the physical or mental state of the defendant which might justify the suspension of his legal responsibilities. In fact, he found Woyzeck to be healthy, earnest, rational, unexpectedly articulate, attentive, responsive, and above average in native intelligence. He found him of average stature and without abnormal features except for a slightly enlarged right testicle. The impression of perfect normalcy was only slightly marred by Woyzeck's unusually severe trembling during the first few minutes of each session in the examination room. This condition was ascribed by Clarus to temporary irregularities of the circulatory system. While the trembling was going on, he noticed irregularities in the heartbeat and a rapid pulse. Once the defendant had calmed down, however, his heartbeat and pulse returned to normal, leading the examiner to diagnose a predisposition toward, but no actual manifestation of, a circulatory disease.

In the defendant's spiritual development, Clarus did discover some defects: "The traces of religious feelings he [Woyzeck] sometimes expresses . . . are too . . . weak to attribute to them any influence over his thoughts and actions," the physician observed. But most pronounced, and especially disturbing to Clarus because they contrasted so sharply with his otherwise highly favorable impressions of the man, were "the symptoms of moral decadence, of blunted natural feelings, and of indifference toward the present and the future."[3]

Thus the defendant emerged from his examination with the best possible recommendation for the death penalty. The reasons for the many failures in life—turned up by Clarus' somewhat superficial investigation of Woyzeck's background—were not to be found either in physical impairments or in mental handicaps. If anywhere, they had to be sought in the inadequacies of his motivational impulses. But the absence of a deep and abiding religious faith, the lack of strong moral convictions, the paralysis of "natural" emotions, and the attitude of indifference toward life, no matter how severely pronounced such defects might be, could not mitigate the defendant's responsibility before the law.

Inevitably, Clarus' report led to the conviction of the defendant. The public defender filed an appeal to have the findings of the report corroborated by a second examiner. It, as well as two subsequent appeals for mercy, was rejected. Woyzeck was sentenced to death by the sword. The execution was scheduled for November 13, 1822. Three days before that date, however, the court issued another stay. A private citizen had filed a petition in behalf of Woyzeck, and the court wanted to have the opportunity to test its merits. Apparently motivated by the continuing controversy in the press, this good Samaritan in the cause of justice had personally investigated the convict's background. By talking with former landlords, employers, fellow workers, roommates, neighbors, storekeepers, comrades, etc., he had uncovered very strong evidence of a serious mental disease. Woyzeck had mentioned hallucinations to a number of people. Phantom voices had spoken to him. He had been observed rolling on the floor shouting, "I'm lost, I'm lost." One landlord had seen him pacing up and down the stairway muttering, "Here it comes." A voice commanding him, "Jump into the water," came to light. There were reports of long periods of unresponsiveness marked by a vacant stare. At a cemetery he had heard people talk when there was no one there. He had spoken of conversations between ghosts in his room. Fear of the freemasons who—so he had claimed—were chasing him because he had learned some of their secrets by accident, had sometimes made him suddenly run away or adopt grotesque defensive gestures.

The court, by issuing its highly dramatic stay of execution, clearly demonstrated that it was impressed with the new evidence. All the more serious was the error that was now made in the proceedings. Instead of calling an uncommitted physician to re-examine the defendant at this point, as the defense was insisting, the judge reappointed Dr. Clarus, who saw his reputation at stake. It is hardly surprising that his findings after five more sessions with the defendant corroborated his original opinions. That he was, himself, not totally insensitive to the question of propriety in this procedure is indicated by the fact that, on his own initiative, he took his new report to the medical school for its endorsement. Although this endorsement probably involved little more than a rubber stamping by some of his associates at the university, it had the effect of overawing the court despite the fact that it was a far less convincing document than the first report. What judge would be willing to question a document which bears the official seal of approval of such a formidable institution as a school of medicine? Despite the continuing public clamor, all further pleas and petitions were brushed aside. The legal proceedings had taken up more than three years. In the case of a self-confessed murderer, who was, besides, the most insignificant of all insignificant men, that was considered long enough. As a result, the City of Leipzig celebrated its first public decapitation in over a generation on August 27, 1824. Some of the spectators were surprised by the small flow of blood from the truncated neck of Johann Woyzeck.

Clarus' second report was considerably longer than the first. It offered a much more detailed account of Woyzeck's background and, therefore, was of great value to Büchner as a source. But as a scientific document it leaves something to be desired. Instead of coming to grips with the newly uncovered information, Clarus launched a multi-pronged attack upon its relevance. First he subtly tries to discredit some of the evidence. For example, he suggests that it was the summer heat, not terror in the face of strange visions, that caused the man to dash out of his room in the middle of the night on several occasions. For those of his readers who nevertheless wanted to take Woyzeck's hallucinations seriously, he develops a series of very slippery arguments seemingly meant to overwhelm rather than convince. For example, he wanted to make Woyzeck's strange behavior patterns seem more normal by associating them with the previously observed circulatory irregularities. The defendant's aberrations were rather typical mental manifestations not uncommonly associated with certain kinds of blood disorders, so he argued. Woyzeck had himself mentioned chest pains and other symptoms of such diseases in talking about his past. The inference is clear: Woyzeck was suffering from a circulatory disease which might have caused his hallucinations. But Clarus was not unaware of the dangers of this inference. The impression of a man helplessly victimized by the vagaries of his blood is exactly what he wanted to avoid. So, instead of drawing the conclusion that logic demands, he simply reminded his readers that his physical examination of the defendant had revealed only the predisposition but no actual organic evidence of such diseases. Incredibly, the argument ultimately collapses into a new diagnosis: Woyzeck suffered from hypochondria. To his credit, it must be pointed out that Clarus did not exactly spell out the feeble implications of this conception, namely, that Woyzeck's phantom visions were not the *real* hallucinations associated with *real*, organic blood diseases, but the *imaginary* hallucinations related to an *imagined* disease.

But Clarus did not leave it at that. He developed yet another, totally unrelated, line of argument to demonstrate the irrelevance of the evidence of insanity laid before the court. Even if it is assumed that Woyzeck did suffer the hallucinations attributed to him—so Clarus reasoned now, in effect—that still did not prove insanity. "To be sure," he wrote, "madness and insanity are governed by illusions and errors in judgment, but not everyone who has illusions and makes errors in judgment is insane." This speculation takes on almost Büchneresque dimensions when Clarus goes on to indicate that the category of the *deluded but still not insane*, within which he would like to count Woyzeck, by no means represents a small minority of mentally underdeveloped or superstitious people. He means to include most, if not all, normal people, if the example he uses to demonstrate the concept is taken at face value. "The opinion that the sun rotates about the earth," he claims, "is based upon a delusion of the senses which, for thousands of years, has led the best minds to mistaken judgments and false conclusions and even today is never doubted for a moment by millions of rational people."[4] This example would serve better to illustrate Büchner's skepticism regarding the reliability of the human senses, for it is doubtful that even Clarus himself belonged to that category of men whose sensory perceptions tell them that the earth is moving about the sun. It takes a rare person indeed to see *earth drop*—five hundred years of enlightenment haven't even developed a name for the daily phenomenon—instead of sunrise in the morning. But Clarus was not a skeptic; he used this argument simply to get himself back to his strongest suit. Illusions, even if they are called hallucinations, do not in themselves prove insanity. With this conclusion he returned to the more solid ground of his first report. Neither mentally nor physically could he regard Woyzeck as abnormal. If the man nevertheless failed in life, his failures could only be explained by the inadequacies of his religious convictions and motivational impulses, and by his cold indifference toward the world and toward himself.

In his summation, Clarus inexplicably returns to the question of irregularities in the prisoner's blood circulation which he had himself discarded, albeit somewhat clumsily, elsewhere in the report. Was it perhaps that he felt somewhat uncertain within himself about this issue? The world will never know, but, in a postscript added for the second publication of the document, Clarus held up the results of the autopsy as confirmation of the clean bill of health he had given the defendant: Except for a large amount of fat around the heart, all organs of the head, chest, and abdomen were found to be "in completely healthy condition." After a momentary faltering which suggests that he had forgotten some of his own tortured reasoning on the absence or presence of circulatory disorders, Clarus concluded his summation in absolute agreement with the findings of his earlier report: ". . . There is no reason to assume that he [Woyzeck] at any time in his life, and in particular just before, during, and right after the act of murder committed by him, found himself in a state of mental disturbance, or that he acted in response to any irrepressible, blind, and instinctive compulsion, or that he acted in any way other than out of the normal impulses of passion."[5]

There is, of course, much in Clarus' argumentation that Büchner would—and did—object to. He certainly could not have had much admiration for the man; in fact, the ludicrous figure of the Doctor in the play, that caricature of a medical professor who uses Woyzeck for his crazy experimentations, bears more than a merely coincidental resemblance to him. Clarus' spurious rationalizations and especially his smug arrogance must have repulsed him. Even more offensive to him must have been the banal, moralizing, and self-aggrandizing tone of a preface later added by Clarus and intellectually completely incompatible with the findings of the report itself. Nevertheless, the extraordinarily widespread idea that the play is the product of Büchner's indignation, that it represents a frontal counterattack upon Clarus' theories, that, as Hans Mayer puts it, "the judges are here put on trial," simply cannot be supported.[6] Büchner is not well represented by the almost universal assumption among modern critics that he tried to make his "hero" the victim of purely external, mostly social, but sometimes cosmic, forces. The standard conception is that he used the historical incident to develop an answer to that question he had once posed in a letter and later put into Danton's mouth: "What is it in us that lies, whores, steals, and murders?"[7]

A variety of answers to this question have been cited by interpreters of *Woyzeck* as constituting the central theme of the play. It is ironic that precisely those critics who search out a sociological basis for the tragedy place the greatest emphasis on this question. Few seem to take notice of the fact that it very pointedly does not ask, what is it *in our society* or *in our world* that makes us murder, but, "What is it *in us* that . . . murders." Is there any less ambiguous, clearer, and more direct way of saying that the forces which drive us to lie, whore, steal, and kill reside within us than by posing this very question? Despite the clarity, the explanations for Woyzeck's crime pour forth from the pages of the critical interpretations. Mayer seizes upon "poverty, the circumstances of his [Woyzeck's] material life."[8] Lindenberger sees Woyzeck as "victimized in every way conceivable—by his poverty, his social degradation, his mistress' faithlessness, his rival's brutality, and his frightening mental visions."[9] Knight reads the play as a kind of "essay" on "how men are *driven* to commit crimes . . ." (his emphasis).[10] Viëtor's position, much more hedged on this issue, nevertheless also seeks the explanation outside rather than inside the "hero." "Woyzeck's fate is guided by a turbid necessity which dominates life and does not concern itself with the will or conscience of individual people," he writes.[11] But it is not only that the answers supposedly found in the play are irrelevant to the question, it is also the very expectation that the play should contain any answer at all that makes this kind of approach highly dubious. Büchner had placed the question in a letter because he could think of no answers to it, and the clear implication of Danton's use of the question is that there is no answer to it. Could not Büchner immediately have thought of such cliché-ridden conceptions as *poverty, social degradation, jealousy,* or *fate* if his curiosity was to be so easily satisfied? Such a question, after all, is directed to the gods, and Büchner was anything but certain that there was a God to hear it. Far more convincing would be the idea that the question, in its real meaning, was the theme of the play. But, just as in *Danton,* the answer here is left to the gods. My God, what is it in Woyzeck that murders? So far no answer has been found, but the question hangs over the play like a pall. Countless details of Woyzeck's inner and outer life are revealed. We know how he talks, thinks, and works; we know his gestures, his feelings, his fears, his visions; we know what he yearns for and what oppresses him; we know who he is and perhaps even why he is; we know a great deal about him, but we cannot understand what it is in him that murders. Knowing so much and yet not knowing, therein lies the tragedy! And it was not really Büchner who created the tragedy. It was Johann Woyzeck who lived it, and it was that self-righteous, rather priggish doctor from Leipzig who first discovered it. Clarus, too, failed to find an answer to the question of why Woyzeck killed. He unearthed a wealth of information about his background, about his state of mind, about his likes and dislikes, about the way he moved and gestured, about the way he thought; he looked in his ears, his throat, his anus, but nowhere could he find the answer. He did find many reasons why Woyzeck did not murder. He did not murder because of his bad circulation, he did not murder because he was insane, stupid, irrational, lazy, or drunk. Clarus does not say that he did not murder because he was poor or because of his social degradation, but if he had thought about it, he undoubtedly would have indicated that too, for despite all the reasons for which Woyzeck did not kill, Woyzeck did kill.

A momentary digression is necessary at this point. In the previously mentioned preface to his report, Clarus did speculate about motivations for the crime. However, these speculations stand in direct conflict with the findings of the report proper. The special purpose of the preface offers at least a partial explanation for the inconsistencies. The Leipzig authorities, fearful of popular demonstrations on behalf of the condemned man, decided to publish Clarus' second report a week before the execution. Apparently it was felt that wider understanding of the case would dissipate the compassion which could lead to unseemly incidents on execution day. The last previous decapitation ceremony had been marred by embarrassing expressions of sympathy. Women had strewn flowers, and someone had decorated the scaffold with a sign reading, "Sleep gently, good Jonas." Obviously Clarus was asked to write his preface with the special problem in mind. Seemingly approaching this new task with relish and with true dedication to the principle of what he himself called the "invulnerable sanctity of the law," he used the opportunity to preach banal moral lessons to his readers. Perhaps assuming (probably correctly so) that few would ever read the report itself, he puffed himself up and descended like the wrath of a vengeful god upon a despicable sinner. This beast of a man, he said in effect, despite all the opportunities offered him by an enlightened, God-fearing society, has made himself miserably unworthy of any human compassion whatsoever. The change in tone reflects the change in purpose. In the report written for the court he had spoken in the language of his profession. Now, writing for the populace, he affected the language of the pulpit. He adopted the pose of one whose words could not possibly express all the disgust he felt. Completely forgetting the contents of the report, forgetting that it specifically states that Woyzeck was not a lazy man, forgetting that not a word about the defendant's gambling habits had been mentioned there, forgetting that the man had been stone sober when he committed the crime, forgetting numerous notations to the effect that Woyzeck was not sexually promiscuous, that he had, in fact, always tended toward devotion to one woman, forgetting his own description of the man as a shy loner who shunned company—forgetting all that, he reaches the climax of his sermon with a little prayer: "May our young people, upon seeing the bleeding criminal, or upon thinking of him, impress deeply upon their mind this truth: That the aversion to work, gambling, drunkenness, the promiscuous satisfaction of the sex drive, and bad company can eventually lead to crime and the scaffold."[12] Unfortunately, this banal sentence, meant to deceive, has been used by some critics to characterize the main thrust of the report itself. Small wonder that Büchner's play looks to many like an angry attack upon Clarus. After all, his "hero" specifically does not neglect his work, refuses to drink even under the threat of a beating, never gambles, is completely faithful to his Marie, and is a shy loner who shuns company. Where is the resemblance? Perhaps it was only Clarus' prejudice that caused him to find nothing in Woyzeck's character that could explain his extraordinarily vicious crime—seven thrusts of the knife before his anger waned. Perhaps he felt he had to find him innocent to find him guilty. But whatever the reason, it was under his pen that the idea for Büchner's play was born. What could be more terrifying than the idea that not a beast, not a monster, not even a sex fiend or a drunk, but a perfectly gentle, modest, rational, altogether ordinary kind of man, a man not unlike millions of others, should suddenly turn upon another human being and kill—not just kill, but butcher? This idea goes against one of man's most ingrained myths. The devil, the cyclops, the werewolf, the Abominable Snowman, evil spirits of all sorts, Frankenstein's monster, Mr. Hyde, they are all invented by the mind to ward off the unacceptable truth. The myth is represented everywhere; it stares down from gargoyles on buildings and fountains, from paintings, drawings, and sculptures, it comes out of hundreds of books. The thought is always the same: there are monsters walking the earth, and these monsters, rather than humans, commit these hideous crimes that stand beyond comprehension. The legend of the monster attaches itself to all perpetrators of seemingly senseless, or particularly brutal, crimes, not just to the famous ones like Jack the Ripper or the Boston Strangler. Clarus' mind was not exceptional; it, too, was in the grip of the myth. That can be seen in the way he described his first examination of Woyzeck. Besides recording his actual observations, he also noted down what he did not see. The image of the monster first looms up when he points out that Woyzeck's head does *not* have an extraordinary shape, does *not* show any scars or unusual markings. Woyzeck, he indicated, does *not* have stinky breath; his body shows *no* particular rigidity; his skin is free from blemishes; the look in his eyes is "*not at all* wild, insolent, disturbed, unsteady, or confused"; furthermore, his facial expression "has *nothing* deceitful, malicious, repulsive, or uncanny about it, *nor* does it reveal . . . repressed anger," and his smile is *not* "unpleasant, bitter, or mocking."[13] The specter of the monster, the product of the doctor's myth-bound expectations, stands there with its weird head, its fiery breath, its wild eyes, its maliciously gloating facial expression, and its bitter, mocking smile; it stands there right beside Woyzeck. But the scientist in Clarus beat back the myth and brought him face to face with a rather gentle human being and an awful truth. Perhaps it was the inability of his mind to sustain this truth which, along with his priggish concern for public morality, made him slip back into the myth when he sat down to write his preface. Who can long bear the thought that there is something in *us* (that includes *me*) that is capable of the most terrible crimes? The mind demands that something must be found in the criminal to make him different from us. Even Büchner, when the question first occurred to him, followed it in his letter with an escapist's remark: "What is it in us that lies, murders, steals? I don't want to pursue the idea."[14]

But he did pursue the idea. He found in Clarus a clear expression of the truth behind the myth. Perhaps this is the time to ask once more what the real substance of the controversy over the case of Johann Woyzeck was. Was not the debate actually a confrontation between the truth and the myth? Revolting against the idea that Woyzeck was "just like us," the popular conscience demanded that he be branded as being outside the realm of human normalcy. Precisely the fact that there were reports of the man's strange behavior at various times in his life gave the case its special significance. Here were the straws to which the myth could cling. But Clarus did not allow it a foothold, nor did Büchner, for if one thing is certain about Woyzeck it is the fact that it was no illusion, but a very clear insight into realities that preceded the murder. To be sure, just like the historical model, the protagonist of the drama hears a voice demanding, "Stab her dead, stab her dead." But this is not the voice of a ghost, but an echo of his mind; it is the voice of that indeterminable force which resides within him, just as it resides in all of us.

Important as it is, however, Büchner's assault upon the myth of the monster cannot be regarded as the central theme of the play. The fact that Woyzeck kills because that terrible inner force seizes control over him contains deeply tragic implications for mankind, but it is not the basis of his personal tragedy. Woyzeck is more than the loser of a game of Russian roulette—more than simply "a poor, unlucky devil." He not only loses that final deadly game, he loses all the games in life, most of them by default. He cannot even participate, but is, in fact, totally unfit for living. That is his tragedy, and the anatomy of his suffering is the main theme of the play. Before broaching that theme, however, it is necessary to clarify Büchner's relationship to Clarus a little more thoroughly. Woyzeck's unsuitability for life, and even the reasons for it, also stem from this source, but it is not merely the establishment of the connection, but the light it throws upon Büchner's esthetic goals that prompts the interruption of the stream of thought at this point. There is every indication that Büchner approached his historical source with every intention of remaining completely faithful to it. In one of the very few comments he made in his letters concerning the craft of the dramatist, he pointed to the great importance of historical accuracy. The comment (previously discussed in relation to *Danton*) indicated that he saw the dramatist essentially as the second writer of history who creates characters out of characteristics found in historical narrative. Perhaps more important than Büchner's view of the dramatist's role is the conception of history it implies. Proving just how narrowly he could sometimes see the world through the professional eyes of the playwright, he speaks of history not in the then newly popular intellectual terms of colliding forces, of theses and antitheses, nor even in the more mundane terms of actions, facts, places, and developments related to time, but in terms of personages whose essence is expressed in certain personal characteristics. Thus, being faithful to an historical source must have primarily meant to him the accurate retranslation of the "dead" descriptions of historical figures into the "living" figures of the stage.[15] That this rather unusual conception should lead him to seek out very special kinds of historical source materials is hardly surprising. Pastor Oberlin's observations of the day-by-day occurrences in the life of a young poet over a period of some months, upon which Büchner had based his *Lenz*, represent precisely the kind of material he could be expected to look for. The Clarus documents, though very different in other ways, share with Oberlin's descriptions their extraordinarily narrow focus upon the activities and thoughts of a single man. Until the advent of psychological case studies, such detailed, firsthand observations of individuals made and recorded over a considerable period of time were not at all common. There is, then, some reason to suspect that Büchner had not only thematic but also esthetic interests in the Clarus reports. Here was a true challenge to him, the second recorder of history, or the creative recorder, as he liked to think of himself. Could he shape a character out of these characteristics? Could he take that great abundance of dead narrative description and bring it back to life before the theater audience?

There are elements in the form, as well as in the content, of *Woyzeck* which suggest precisely such esthetic considerations. Knight's conception of the play as "an essay in the psychology of murder" is not totally without foundation, for Büchner did preserve some of the formal qualities of his essaylike source.[16] A tone of scientific objectivity has frequently been noted, but it has only rarely been tied to the structure of the play. Perhaps it was C. R. Mueller who made the most telling connection when he wrote: "*Woyzeck* . . . is as dispassionate in any explicit way as a medical lecture. This clarity and sharpness of focus are due in great part to Büchner's practice of fully developing only his major character or characters."[17] As a translator Mueller noticed a rather unique quality that cannot elude anyone who has ever participated in a stage production of the play. *Woyzeck* is essentially a one-man play. Its protagonist is almost constantly on the stage. Only three very brief scenes allow the actor of the title role a brief rest offstage. With *Woyzeck*, Büchner created the theatrical counterpart of the unique narrative perspective he had developed in *Lenz*. All interest is focused upon the "hero," and the audience is never allowed to ponder the fate of the other characters, who are figures only to the extent that their actions and words affect Woyzeck. With unmatched relentlessness, the viewer is forced into confrontation after confrontation with the one man and his struggles to live despite his unfitness for life.

That Clarus' "essay" on Woyzeck has the same unrelenting focus hardly needs to be demonstrated, for that is in the nature of such reports, whose purpose it is to explore the personality of the one man; and, insofar as any mention is made of others, they are only identified by name or profession and in terms of their influence upon his life. Neither their motivations nor their personalities play any role whatsoever. But the idea that Büchner structured his play in accord with the formal peculiarities of his source is of special interest only because it offers an important clue to the nature of the relationship between the play and its

source. The facts transferred from Clarus to Büchner—such
things as Woyzeck's fear of the freemasons, his dismay at being
called "a good man," the circumstances surrounding his purchase
of the knife, his nervous trembling before the imposing person-
age of the Doctor, the inner voice that commands him to kill, his
encounter with Marie dancing in the arms of another man and
whispering those maddening words, "Don't stop, don't stop," his
impulses to throw his weapon into the pond, etc.—have always
been acknowledged. Nor have the obvious differences escaped
notice. Thus, Marie seems to have little in common with the
forty-six-year-old widow whose unenviable role she usurps. Indeed, none of the supporting characters have any really significant roots in the historical document. In the days before Johann
Woyzeck became totally homeless, he had to share a bed in a
loft with a former drum major who was obviously just as unfortunate as he. The routine annotation by Clarus leads Büchner to
invent a Drum Major who shares the woman, not the mattress. And
so it is with the other shadowy figures who populate the stage.
They are Büchner's inventions based upon no more than a hint
in the Clarus text. Officers who are generally described as having
been satisfied with Woyzeck's performance of his duties are
stylized into the single figure of the Captain. While Büchner's
Doctor may resemble Clarus himself in some ways, his activities
are also reminiscent of some of Büchner's professors in Giessen.
To the extent that Büchner does develop figures other than
Woyzeck, he does not hesitate to exercise his imagination. When
it comes to his main figure, however, the freedom he claims elsewhere comes to an end. Apparently, his own conception of the
role of the dramatist vis-à-vis history tolerated practically no
changes here. The dramatic essence of the historical events, according to his theory, resides in the personality of the individuals
involved in them. The absolutely faithful reproduction of the
historical characteristics of those people, and only those people
for whom they have been clearly developed in the source, is more
than a whim, it is a powerful, though, of course, self-imposed,
obligation.

Theoretically, then, Woyzeck's character, but not necessarily
that of the others, should be completely true to that of his
model. And so it is. It would be very difficult indeed to find a
single tone, gesture, or conception in the protagonist which is

not directly related to Clarus' observations. The dialogue, of course, is largely invented (Clarus gave only few indications as to the content of Woyzeck's conversations), yet it consistently expresses ideas rooted in the case history. The same is true of the scene sequence. Büchner orders things the way he sees fit. Details of time and place are liberally rearranged. For example, the murder does not occur at dusk in the entrance hall of Mrs. Woost's house, but at a pond in the light of the moon. Perhaps the most serious discrepancy with the historical material is found in the nature of Woyzeck's relationship to Marie, which is markedly different from the one between the real murderer and his victim. In the play, the two have a child and live more or less as if they were married—without the blessing of the church, of course.

As has been pointed out, the Woyzeck-Woost relationship had been a stormy and ill-defined affair, and there was no child involved. Nevertheless, even this difference cannot be regarded as an inaccuracy in characterization, for the relationship Büchner develops is just as solidly rooted in the historical source. He simply placed the dramatic focus on an earlier period in Woyzeck's life, i.e., on the time when he was still a soldier. In those days, specifically in 1810, according to Clarus, Woyzeck lived with a woman identified only by the name Wienbarg. The two had a child, and he requested permission from his superiors to marry her. The marriage did not take place, for, after a long period of indecisiveness, he deserted her. The episode attracted Clarus' special attention because it was in those same days that Woyzeck reportedly first began to experience the strange sensations and mysterious visions that were to trouble his life from then on.[18] In other words, Clarus, even before Büchner, considered this period a climactic turning point. That Büchner, interested in capturing the essence of Woyzeck's character, should also focus on this highly revealing moment is more than natural. Nevertheless, there is at least one indication that Büchner may have felt some uneasiness about this rather radical rearrangement of events. Creating the dramatist's equivalent of a scholarly footnote, he wrote a scene which has little other purpose than to make the chronological shift explicit. In it, Woyzeck, apparently thinking that his life is about to end, begins to read his own description from his military identification papers and then calculates his age down to the day. Instead of forty-one, he is just over thirty years old, exactly the age of the historical Woyzeck in 1810, when he and the woman named Wienbarg were planning to marry, when he was in the Swedish military service, and when his hallucinations first began to trouble him.

What forms the crucial link between Clarus and Büchner is clearly not the when or where of the actions, but the realistic representation of the interplay of character traits. This is demonstrated in countless ways. Clarus' cold, descriptive language is translated into speech and action. "Shyness" is no longer a word or phrase but a behavior pattern impressed upon the personality of the "hero." "Well-articulated speech," a quality which has occasionally been criticized in the literary characterization by those who insist on seeing a simpleton in Woyzeck, becomes a reality upon the stage. Woyzeck's inquisitiveness, his lack of bitterness toward his rivals and tormentors, his efforts to please, his unmilitary dislike for brawling and carousing with comrades—these are not things talked about but demonstrated. The transformation of such bits of historical information from the language of the essay into the often wordless sign language of the stage represented a technical challenge to the playwright in Büchner. But there was another set of characteristics, those dealing directly with the quality of Woyzeck's mind, where the relationship goes well beyond the dramatist's purely esthetic concerns for historical accuracy.

It would undoubtedly be an exaggeration to speak of an intellectual bond between the two men, but, nevertheless, Büchner found bits of information in Clarus' descriptions which fitted, piece by piece, into his own evolving psychological conceptions. Clarus himself, of course, did not become involved in discussions of psychological theory. Yet it seems clear that he thought in highly traditional terms. To him Woyzeck represented a classic enigma: a man divided against himself. In one place he even spoke of a "being" he had encountered within the prisoner during the first months of his captivity, an "indifferent, cold, raw, and decivilized being."[19] He apparently thought in terms of an inner conflict between certain constructive and destructive forces. On one side were the "positive" qualities, such as intelligence, alertness, earnestness, and rationality; but these were opposed by a mysterious inner being which undermined the defendant's motivational impulses. Woyzeck's weaknesses, his inadequate religious faith, his moral decadence, his blunted emotions, and his indifference toward the world, were the unhappy effects of this inner confrontation. But where Clarus seems to have seen a discomforting inconsistency of character, Büchner undoubtedly recognized an all too familiar, if tragic, harmony. One need only think of *Danton* to understand that precisely such defects as indifference, moral decadence, and blunted senses were, in Büchner's conception, totally consistent with—in fact directly attributable to—what Clarus had considered the positive qualities of the mind. Despite the differences in the diagnosis, the contact is remarkably close. Woyzeck emerges from the historical report with all the symptoms of the typical Büchner "hero" already in evidence. Just as in Oberlin's observations, Büchner found scattered through the Clarus reports all the ingredients that demonstrated the basic validity of his own conception of the human tragedy. Though much distillation was necessary to capture the dramatic essence, very few traits had to be added.

Woyzeck differs from Büchner's earlier works inasmuch as it was written within a still current historical context. The audience for which the play was intended undoubtedly would have understood the relationship to the still controversial case much better than it was understood once the play actually began to reach the public after 1879. Surely it would have been clear to contemporaries that Büchner's conception could not be related to the question of the criminal's guilt or innocence on any of the psychological or legal grounds that had been under discussion at the time, including the position which attacked the validity of Clarus' inadequate scientific methods.[20] People who were familiar with at least some of the particulars of the historical case would have been far less prepared than later generations to see political principles extolled in the play. Taken out of its historical context, and viewed only within the framework of a literary tradition whose tragic heroes at that time were still mostly kings, princes, and other powerful figures from the past or out of the pages of the Bible, the mere idea of a tragedy about the ordeals of poor people by itself suggests a distinct political message. No comparable treatment of material deprivation can be found on the German stage until the advent of naturalism at the end of the nineteenth century. Ironically, however, the moment the play is

viewed against the background of the specific problems related
to the case of Johann Woyzeck, political ideologies begin to fade
in importance. When Büchner reduced the age of the murderer
by eleven years and pictured him in an earlier, more profound
relationship, when he depicted him not as the social reject which
the historical figure finally became but as a soldier who spends
his spare time on all kinds of menial, yet not altogether unrewarding, odd jobs in order to be able to take his Marie to the
carnival, he did this not to emphasize but to soften the political
implications.

Seeing the play too much in terms of the literary tradition and
not enough in relation to its special historical context has led
to rather shallow readings of the text. Sociopolitical interpretations depend heavily upon those few scenes which show Woyzeck interacting with his bosses, the Captain and the Doctor.
From a modern point of view, it is all too easy to see in these
gentlemen rather familiar, by now thoroughly traditionalized,
figures. On the surface, they seem to be easily recognizable as the
typical representatives of an oppressive middle-class establishment. That they are exploiters of the poor, that they try to use
their position of influence and power to corrupt and degrade
Woyzeck who stands meekly and powerlessly below them on
the social ladder—of that there can be no doubt. But is this their
sole, or even main, function in the play? A careful reading of the
text will reveal that it is not. While these two characters do fall
roughly into the same social class, they have very little else in
common. Lumping them into a single category tends to obscure
the fact that they represent not only differing, but conflicting,
views of the world.

The Captain certainly does not speak with the self-assurance
usually associated with bourgeois oppressiveness. His very first
words seem to point in a totally different direction. Sitting in a
chair while Woyzeck shaves him, he tries—unsuccessfully—to
strike up a conversation:

Not so fast, Woyzeck, not so fast! One thing at a time! You're making
me dizzy. What am I to do with the extra ten minutes you'll finish
early today? Just think Woyzeck: you still have thirty beautiful years
to live! Thirty years! That makes three hundred and sixty months!
And days! Hours! Minutes! What do you think you'll do with all that
horrible stretch of time? Have you ever thought about it, Woyzeck?[21]

These are anything but the words of a man at peace with himself. Rather than self-confidence, they express a kind of inner turmoil not at all without precedent among Büchner's dramatic figures. Life, to the Captain, represents an enormous, empty space of time which somehow has to be filled. That Leonce expresses precisely the same idea in only slightly different words cannot escape notice: "My life gapes at me like a vast expanse of white paper I'm to fill, but I can't produce so much as a single letter," he had complained.[22] Could it be, then, that the same debilitating skepticism which had once made life appear so meaningless to Leonce is also gnawing at the soul of the Captain? There is every indication that this is exactly the case. The Captain tries to use Woyzeck just as Leonce had used the fool, Valerio, to provide himself with a momentary respite from his own gloomy thoughts. In direct contrast to the usual representation of the solid burgher who conceives of time as one of the most holy commodities, the Captain's major preoccupation seems to be the problem of making time slip by as painlessly as possible. The activity of the world around him seems, to him, devoid of all meaning, as his very next words indicate:

It frightens me when I think about the world, when I think about eternity. Busyness, Woyzeck, busyness! There's the eternal: that's eternal, that is eternal. That you can understand. But then again it's not eternal. It's only a moment. Woyzeck, it makes me shudder when I think that the earth turns itself about in a single day! What a waste of time! Where will it all end? Woyzeck, I can't even look at a mill wheel anymore without becoming melancholy.

On the surface, the Captain's babbling is, of course, nonsensical. However, meaningless as it is to Woyzeck, it is not insignificant to the audience, for it lays bare the misfunctions of a mind tormented by its inability to grasp the meaning inherent in the activities of man and nature, in the eternal, but then again only momentary, "busyness" going on around him, as he himself puts it. Dizziness (mentioned in the previously quoted passage), fear, and melancholy—these are the psychological effects of his confrontation with reality; to avoid them he shies back from life, withdraws into himself, becomes a kind of human vegetable as the Doctor notes in a scene to be discussed momentarily. But even within himself there is no peace. His ideas turn one against the other. Eternity is not eternity, it is only a moment, but then again maybe it is eternal after all. The speed of the rotating earth makes him shudder, but then again he thinks of all the time wasted by that motion. Instead of meshing, his thoughts come in clashing contrasts.

In a few strokes, Büchner sketches the image of a man whose mind is functionally paralyzed. Every thought suggests its opposite, thereby annihilating all meaning. The juxtaposition of opposites even forms the basis of a little joke he wants to play on Woyzeck, who dutifully responds to all the nonsensical wisdom with the conventional military "yes, sir." The Captain tells him that the wind is blowing out of the *north-south* and then waits for the inevitable "yes, sir," so he can have a laugh at the soldier's expense. But his amusement quickly turns into bitterness and then into maudlin sentimentality: "Ha! Ha! Ha! North-south! Ha! Ha! Ha! Oh he's a stupid one! Horribly stupid! [*Moved.*] Woyzeck you are a good man, but [*With dignity.*] Woyzeck, you have no morality!" Along with his extraordinarily swift changes of mood, stressed by the stage directions, the battle of opposing ideas continues. The Captain sees Woyzeck as horribly stupid; but, then, maybe he is not stupid, but good; but, then, again he isn't really good either, but immoral. "You have a child without the blessings of the church," the Captain points out to substantiate the immorality charge, but then he goes on to discard this notion as well. It was not his own idea, he claims, but he was only repeating what the chaplain had been saying.

So that no one might misunderstand the significant aspects of the Captain's weird mentality and take him to be the ordinary kind of preachy moralist that many critics have nevertheless discovered in him, Büchner repeats the whole charade once more, this time in reverse order.[23] Demonstrating the consistency of his inconsistency, the Captain begins with the proposition, "Woyzeck, you have no virtue," and ultimately deduces from this that he is "a good man, a good man." Büchner makes no attempt to develop the Captain's personality fully. The heavy, almost tragic, undertone of his philosophizing about time and the activities of the world gives way to a much lighter tone, bordering on the grotesquely comic, when he begins his mental gyrations about morality. But even when he is teasing, his thoughts lack coherence. His passivity extends even into his sexual consciousness. Love, he maintains, is what he feels when he is resting by the window when it rains, watching the white stockings scurrying along the street. Not unlike Danton, he survives only because he fears death even more than the emptiness of life. That becomes evident in the scene marked "Street," where he meets the Doctor.[24] But the primary purpose of this scene, one of the very few that show an interaction between supporting characters, is to emphasize and clarify the nature of the differences between these two gentlemen. That this is hardly a friendly meeting between two mutually respectful social peers is self-evident from the beginning. The Doctor is in a hurry; the Captain, grabbing hold of his coat tails, forces him to slow down so he can consult him professionally about his problems: "Doctor, I'm so melancholy, I have such fantasies. I start to cry every time I see my coat hanging on the wall," he complains.[25] The Doctor, not afflicted with the Captain's indecisiveness, makes an on-the-spot diagnosis: "Hm! Bloated, fat, thick neck: apoplectic constitution. Yes, Captain, you'll be having apoplexia cerebria any time now. . . . If things go really well you'll be mentally disabled so you can vegetate away the rest of your days. You may look forward to something approximately like that within the next four weeks." Though severe doubts have already been cast upon the Doctor's medical judgment in an earlier scene, his gloating apprehension about the Captain's brain is more than a grotesque episode within the framework of the play. On the one hand, there is a man whose life has dissolved into a state of more or less permanent melancholia, whose sense of reality consists of a series of disjointed visions which he cannot bring into any kind of coherent focus, a man who cannot place even the simplest ideas into meaningful relationships to one another. And, pitted against him, there is the "scientist," a man to whom everything seems perfectly clear, who has the answers to all problems, who has such confidence in his learning that he can make instant diagnoses of future diseases based on no more evidence than the dimensions of a neck. "Mr. Hollowhead" and "Mr. Simplistic" they helpfully call each other in the next exchange.[26] Perhaps if they had been labeled Mr. Nihilism and Mr. Positivism the point of the play would have been clear to all. But the actual labels do not seem to be so difficult to decipher. On one side there is the empty-headed skeptic who has no answers to anything; on the other side there is Dr. Positivism, the dogmatist who is smugly satisfied with the simplistic answers he has in store for every occasion.

The important point is that Woyzeck is not shown against the background of a monolithic social order. That the tension between the two representatives of that order is neither social nor political is self-evident. Just as in *Danton*, the establishment breaks into two camps, defined largely in psychological terms. In the one camp there are the "productive" thinkers, the Robespierres, the Saint-Justs, and the Doctors, the "healthy" and faithful believers in human purposes and progress. They judge reality on the basis of appearances, filling in the gaps with myth and what Valerio in *Leonce and Lena* calls "a commodious religion." Nature, to them, represents the origin from which man has risen, and domination over it is his sacred mission. In the other camp there are the sick ones, the Dantons, the Leonces, and the Captains, the ones made dizzy by the earth seeming to spin aimlessly through space. Their search for a deeper meaning in life causes them to falter into a desperate nihilism. They learn to distrust appearances, refuse to bridge the gaps between dream and reality with mythologies, and consequently regard themselves, indeed all mankind, as tragically missionless wanderers. Man's "rise above" nature looks to them rather more like a cruel ejection from the womb. Like the little orphan in the tale told by the old Grandmother in *Woyzeck*, they are cast adrift in an essentially empty world. Only the stars in the sky seem to be real, but when they reach out for the sun or the moon they find that these heavenly bodies, too, are but meaningless illusions.[27] As the Captain himself realizes all too well when he stares at his coat hanging on the wall, nothing but tears are left for such disillusioned children.

The Grandmother's tale is, of course, an allegorical representation not of the Captain's but of Woyzeck's fate. It is this particular orphan's desperate struggle to maintain faith in his tarnished stars which forms the main theme of the play. But the figures of the Captain and the Doctor provide the intellectual framework within which this struggle takes place. Büchner leaves open only two paths to human exploration, one that leads to the despairing vision into the emptiness of existence, and the other, holding out the promise of contentment and even happiness, leads through mythologies and blind faith to conceptions which the travelers on this path mistakenly, but perhaps fortunately, identify as knowledge. Just how wrong those people are who rest in the security of their "knowledge" becomes instantly clear in that brilliantly conceived scene, "At the Doctor's":

DOCTOR: I don't believe it Woyzeck! And a man of your word!
WOYZECK: What's that, Doctor sir?
DOCTOR: I saw it all, Woyzeck. You pissed on the street! You were pissing on the wall like a dog! And here I'm giving you three groschen a day plus board! That's terrible Woyzeck! The world's becoming a terrible place!
WOYZECK: But, Doctor, sir, when Nature . . .
DOCTOR: When Nature? When Nature? What has Nature to do with it? Did I or did I not prove that the *musculus constrictor vesicae* is controlled by the will? Nature! Woyzeck, man is free! In mankind alone we see glorified the individual's will to freedom! And you couldn't hold your water! [28]

The most fundamental error of the knower (the "scientist") comes into focus here. Surely there is no one alive who cannot feel, within his own organs, the ludicrous wrongness of the Doctor's "proof" of the human will's control over the *musculus constrictor vesicae*. Shocking as it is on the stage even today, Büchner could not have chosen a clearer symbol to drive home the point of his argument. No amount of reasoning could better demonstrate man's precarious position vis-à-vis nature. Although the human will certainly does exercise some control over the muscle under discussion, the strict limitations of these powers are evident to all. [29] Behind the Doctor's chatter about will power, a rather precise, almost painful message comes across the boards. Rather than making man the master over nature, the human intellect—the very quality which distinguishes him from the "lower" animals like the dogs "pissing on the wall"—is only strong enough to bring him into a most unfortunately disharmonious relationship with it. The image of man that emerges is that of a rebelliously stubborn, but still heavily shackled, slave who sometimes, in his fantasies, mistakenly thinks that, simply because he has the power to think, *he* is the master and *nature* the servant.

The Doctor's path, the one which, in contrast to the Captain's, leads to the affirmation of life, quickly reveals its pitfalls to the audience. The scientific laboratory is not used to unearth the secrets of nature but to twist reality into the contorted shapes required for the confirmation of completely absurd theories. The Doctor gives Woyzeck three groschen a day to eat nothing but peas hoping to make some sort of specimen out of him by means of which he could then create a scientific revolution. "I'm going to blow it (the scientific establishment) sky high," he shouts in expectation. "Urea Oxygen, Ammonium hydrochloratem hyperoxidic. Woyzeck, couldn't you just try to piss again?" When, in another scene, the Doctor throws a cat from a window in order to demonstrate another of his weird conceptions to a class of medical students, he points to the cat's unwillingness to cooperate in the experiment—the frightened animal runs away instead of submitting to the examination—as proof that "animals . . . simply have no scientific instincts."[30] What he actually demonstrates is the utter pointlessness of the "scientific instinct," which, in its eternal restlessness, leads man ever further from the womb, into ever greater disharmony with his surroundings, and ever closer to the abyss.

Whereas the Doctor and the Captain between them define the potentials of the human intellect, Büchner uses comparisons to animals to establish the idea that man's highly developed brain actually represents a kind of biological defect. In these comparisons, he refers almost exclusively to the so-called "intelligent" animals—dogs, cats, monkeys, and horses—which man, through training methods, has been able to bring under partial domination. They are the *denatured* animals who themselves are touched by the human tragedy. Insofar as they display "human" characteristics, they too are freaks walking between heaven and earth. This idea becomes the basis of the two separate carnival scenes (Scenes IV and V in Mueller). The fact that Büchner, despite his obvious concern for literary economy, goes through two expositions of the theme underscores the importance of its message.[31] First comes the scene in front of the fair booth. A carnival pitchman uses a monkey dressed in a costume to draw people into his sideshow. This is his spiel:

Gentlemen, gentlemen! You see before you a creature as God created it! But it is nothing this way! Absolutely nothing! But now look at what Art can do. It walks upright. Wears coats and pants. And even carries a saber. This monkey here is a regular soldier. So what if he isn't much different! So what if he is still on the bottom of the human ladder! Hey there, take a bow! That's the way! Now you are a baron, at least. Give us a kiss! [*The monkey trumpets.*] This little customer is musical, too. . . .[32]

On one level the monkey's rapid climb up the "human ladder" makes a mockery of man and his achievements, but on another, more profound, level the fate of the monkey itself is mocked, for the human talents it displays can lead no further than into its role as the member of the cast of a carnival freak show. Removed from its natural habitat, the monkey becomes a strange curiosity indeed, for to be a successful performer it must, at the same time, still be just "a creature as God created it," and also a creature in feeble rebellion against its origins. Büchner's point is not just that monkeys resemble people, and people, monkeys. The comparison is made not with the healthy monkeys in the jungle, but with the sick, *denatured* specimens that blow trumpets in carnival side-shows. But the metaphor is even more clearly defined when it is carried over into the next scene. Inside the fair booth it is the "astronomical horse," not the monkey, who is the star performer; but the metaphor is the same:

PROPRIETOR OF THE BOOTH [*bringing forward a horse*]: Show your talent! Show your brute reason! Put human society to shame! Gentlemen, this animal you see here, with a tail on its torso, and standing on four hoofs, is a member of all the learned societies—as well as a professor at our university where he teaches students how to ride and fight. But that requires simple intelligence. Now think with your double reason! What do you do when you think with your double reason? Is there a jackass in this learned assembly? [*The nag shakes its head*]. How's that for double reasoning? . . . This is no dumb animal. This is a person! A human being! But still an animal. A beast. [*The nag conducts itself indecently.*] That's right, put society to shame. As you can see, this animal is still in a state of Nature. Not ideal Nature, of course! Take a lesson from him! But ask your doctor first, it may prove highly dangerous! What we have been told by this is: Man must be natural! You are created of dust, sand, and dung. Why must you be more than dust, sand, and dung? Look there at his reason. He can figure even if he can't count on his fingers. . . . A metamorphosed human being.[33]

Woyzeck

Reason as well as "double reason" (apparently the capacity to deceive for the sake of flattery), the very qualities that make the horse into a "person," are also the qualities which break its ideal relationship to nature. The image of man emerging from this rather complex metaphor is perhaps best summed up by the term "not ideal," or—as a more literal translation of the German text would have it—"unideal Nature." Like all other creatures, man is created of dust, sand, and dung, but it is his misfortune that these elements have been combined within him in such a way as to cause him to deny, or even to forget, his origins and, as a result, lose himself in a strange world of his own making which he calls society.

Charlatans and fools are Büchner's spokesmen within the play. They appear out of nowhere and disappear after they deliver their speeches. As a dramatic device, such techniques are not untraditional, but in *Woyzeck* the practice is unusually closely tied to the substance of the messages thus propounded. Who else but mockers can hold the mirror up to such a society. In a world so devoid of human values, truth can only come from liars and madmen. It is, then, not surprising that the final, and most incisive, definition of the human condition comes from a young worker whose intellect is numbed by alcohol. "My soul, my soul stinketh of brandywine," he shouts before climbing upon a table in the dance hall to deliver a mock sermon. It comes at the very moment when Woyzeck sees Marie in the arms of the Drum Major, at the very moment when wishful doubts turn into terrible certainty. In other words, the speech can be considered the dramatic climax of the play. Adopting the language of the Bible, the young man poses mankind's most fundamental question:

I say unto you, forget not the wanderer who standeth leaning against the stream of time, and who giveth himself answer with the wisdom of God, and saith: What is Man? What is Man? Yea, verily I say unto you: How should the farmer, the cooper, the shoemaker, the doctor, live, had not God created Man for their use? How should the tailor live *if He had not implanted the feelings of modesty in Man, and what of the soldier, how should he live* had not God endowed Man with the need to slaughter himself.[34]

With devastating cynicism Büchner again points to the lack of purpose in human existence. Man is created for no other reason

than to give farmers and doctors, perhaps even writers, something to do with all that time they have on their hands. Büchner's words speak for themselves and need no elaboration here.

It is a grotesquely absurd world with which Büchner frames
his version of the controversial murder case, but it is a frame he
needed in order to give meaning to that which had seemed
meaningless not only to Dr. Clarus and his allies, but also to the
opposite camp. With a few powerful images he first undermines,
and then overturns, the value system upon which both sides had
based their arguments. In a world where man's purpose in life is
to keep the shoemaker in business, where the human brain is an
oversophisticated mechanism without real function, where the
power of reason represents a deformity of nature; in a world
whose mysteries defy the freakish "scientific instinct" of man,
and which turns brooding army captains into weeping nihilists—
in such a world, the struggles of Johann Woyzeck to keep the
faith are not at all difficult to comprehend. In fact, in such a
world those struggles come to symbolize the most fundamental
problems every man faces in life. Perhaps Büchner's expansion
of the murderer's name to Friedrich Johann Franz Woyzeck—
giving him the three most popular German first names—was intended to emphasize the broader significance of the story.

Woyzeck's tragedy in Büchner's conception is the tragedy of
every man who opens his eyes and begins to think. His tragic
flaw does not escape the notice of the people closest to him. The
Captain is perhaps speaking from experience when he tells Woyzeck straight out: "You're a good man, a good man. But you think
too much."[35] The Doctor, too, takes note of this dangerous habit
when he points out to him: "Woyzeck, you're philosophizing
again."[36] But it is Marie who foresees the real danger: "He'll go
mad if he keeps thinking that way," she senses.[37] And his comrade Andres, noticing his constant restlessness, calls him a "fool"
for not being able to block off his thoughts. But cursed with the
"scientific instinct," Woyzeck cannot stop thinking. A force within
him demands clarification. He looks for it everywhere: "It's in
the toadstools," he tells the Doctor at one point. "Did you ever
see the shapes the toadstools make when they grow up out of
the earth? If only somebody could read what they say."[38] He
senses meaning in the patterns which nature lays out before him,
but he knows that man does not have the capacity to decipher

[122]

them. To know the languages of the fungi, of the plants and animals, that is Woyzeck's ideal, that is the star for which he is groping, but his striving is in vain, for he is but a man.

Even more perplexing to him than ordinary nature is what he calls "double nature," apparently forming the concept under the influence of the carnival man's expression "double reason." It is "double nature" when nature breaks its own patterns to thwart man: "Like when the sun stops at noon," he says, "and it's like the world was going up in fire." The Doctor, always ready with his explanation, diagnoses Woyzeck's tendency to philosophize in such terms as *idée fixe*. The irony, of course, is that he himself, and not Woyzeck, suffers from fixed ideas. As usual when the Doctor expresses an opinion, just the opposite is true. A comfortable *idée fixe* is exactly what poor Woyzeck lacks.

If he could only find a "commodious religion" like Leonce, anything that he could put blind faith in, then perhaps he could save himself. But how can he sustain faith in a Christian God who causes his creatures to suffer so much? "Our kind is miserable only once: in this world and the next," he says in response to the Captain's nonsensical needling about morality. "I think if we ever got to Heaven we'd have to help with the thunder." This statement has undeniable political overtones. Woyzeck is not as stupid as the Captain thinks; he can see that Christianity is a "commodious religion" only for the rich who preach banal moralities and use the concept of the next world to frighten and suppress the poor and create for themselves a heaven on earth. But far more important than Woyzeck's realization that the church is an oppressive tool in the hands of the rich is the effect of this insight upon his psyche. It is a tragic, not only an angry, insight, for it robs him of the crutch he so desperately needs. Illusion or not, if he is to survive, he needs a strong belief in a beautiful afterlife. But his mind will not let him take comfort in the dream of paradise. To use the metaphor of the Grandmother's tale once more, how could he, the little child all alone in the world, put his faith in a moon which is nothing but a piece of rotten wood?

Neither the church's romanticism of the spirit, nor the Doctor's romanticism of the laboratory, can generate the *idée fixe* which might give comfort to Woyzeck's restless mind. But there is one star in the heavens that outshines all the others, one dream, one ray of hope to which Woyzeck clings for dear life. It is the romanticism of love, the bond that unites him with Marie. That is holy to him, upon that foundation he has built his life. As long as he can believe in this dream, he can tolerate all the degradation, all the toil that fate can heap upon him. But, as the audience very quickly learns, Woyzeck's romantic conception of love as the inseparable union of two people joined together by the forces of nature within man is as fallacious as the Doctor's theory about man's control over the *musculus constrictor vesicae.* Here, too, nature will not be controlled and made to conform to the patterns of human dreams. Nature is the master and man the servant: what it joins together it can tear asunder. And so it is that Woyzeck cannot win his struggle, that his last dream also must be shattered. Not unlike the Doctor, he tries to maintain the illusion by averting his gaze from the truth:

WOYZECK: What's that?
MARIE: Nothing.
WOYZECK: There's something shiny in your hands.
MARIE: An earring. I found it.
WOYZECK: I never have luck like that! Two at a time!
MARIE: Am I human or not!
WOYZECK: I'm sorry, Marie. Look at the boy asleep.[39]

Despite the evidence, he tries to maintain his faith in the romantic myth. He turns to the sleeping child. Does not its existence prove the validity of his belief? For the moment, he suppresses his doubts. But not for long. His "scientific instinct," his drive to seek the truth no matter what the cost, forces him to open his eyes. He begins to follow Marie about and inevitably comes to that insight which does him in. His one remaining ideal crumbles before his eyes. He awakens from his dream and recognizes it for what it was: only a grand illusion. And since all his hopes had been staked upon this one illusion, he finds himself standing at the very edge of the abyss: "Every man's a chasm," he now realizes; "it makes you dizzy when you look down."[40] Suddenly the stark emptiness of human existence yawns before him, and the effect of this revelation upon him is not so different from its effects upon the Captain. The view from the brink is dizzying.

But Woyzeck is not the Captain, he is a poor man who has

to sweat and toil for his right to existence. He cannot afford to idle away "that horrible stretch of time" resting by the window, watching the white stockings flitting by. So even this melancholy alternative is denied him. Though poverty is hardly the cause of his suffering, it does close the last practical, if altogether unenviable, escape route from the total desperation which now seizes him in its icy grip. "The cold indifference toward the present and the future," which had caught Dr. Clarus' special attention in the personality of the historical murderer, is anything but a disharmonious element, as Büchner sees it. On the contrary, it is precisely because Woyzeck has a fundamentally sound mind that he lapses into a state of fatal apathy. It is his active intellect that destroys him. While he shares with all the others the purposelessness of human existence, it is the cruel revelation of this truth that leads him to the edge, and ultimately into the depth, of the chasm.

Marie is sketched along far more traditional lines. She seems to be cut from the same cloth as the Storm and Stress heroines of the 1770's. Like so many of them, she is "a child of nature," under the control of her momentary impulses. Goethe's Gretchen from *Faust* is frequently mentioned as a precurser, and indeed, there are some resemblances.[41] Another Marie, the one in J. M. R. Lenz's *Die Soldaten,* also comes to mind, particularly because she also had become ensnared in the military style of life. But whereas nature was idealized by the Storm and Stress writers, Büchner had "unideal nature" in mind when he created his Marie. She is swept off her feet by the Drum Major who "walks like a lion," but the storm within her gives way to the self-reproaching scruples of her mind: "I *am* bad, I *am!* I could run myself through with a knife! Oh, what a life, what a life! We'll all end up in hell, anyway, in the end: man (and) woman. . . ."[42] Like the "astronomical horse" she is a beast and yet still a human being. Her intellect, her desire to be "good," to be more than "dust, sand, and dung," makes her as untrue to her "nature" as the beast within her makes her become untrue to her mission as Woyzeck's woman. She, too, is a tragic figure, but her role, as indeed the roles of all the women in Büchner's plays, is completely passive.

One way out of the human dilemma is left open by Büchner. It offers only temporary refuge for the mind, but nevertheless is not dismissed as altogether frivolous. Woyzeck hears about it from his friend Andres when the latter tells him to take "some schnapps with a powder in it." But the Drum Major delivers the message to him much more forcefully:

I'm a man! [*He pounds his chest.*] A man, you hear? Anybody say different? Anybody who's not as crocked as the Lord God himself better keep off. I'll screw his nose up his ass! [*To Woyzeck*] You there, get drunk! I wish the world were schnapps, schnapps! You better start drinking! [*Woyzeck whistles.*] Son-of-a-bitch, you want me to pull your tongue out and wrap it around your middle? [*They wrestle; Woyzeck loses.*] You want I should leave you enough wind for a good old lady's fart? Uh! [*Exhausted and trembling, Woyzeck seats himself on a bench.*] The son-of-a-bitch can whistle himself blue in face for all I care. [*Sings.*]

> Brandy's my life, my life
> Brandy gives me courage.[43]

Despite the clarity of the message, Woyzeck does not listen. Just as he rejects the intoxicating theories of the Doctor which make the world seem so orderly, so he now rejects the Drum Major's forceful invitation to blot out the unbearable truth by drinking.[44] But alcohol is the only prescription Büchner can offer to cure, at least temporarily, the human condition. In his constant state of intoxication, the Drum Major finds life quite bearable. His relationship to Marie contrasts sharply with Woyzeck's. There are no illusions, no feelings of attachment; there is no family instinct, no spiritual bond, but only the urge to still a powerful animal passion. Here is the means to make the return to nature possible. With enough brandy, "unideal nature" can be turned into ideal nature. Deaden the intellect, and nature will set you free. That is Büchner's bitter advice, and it is not sheer mockery, for a tone of desperate seriousness can be detected in the words of a drunken young worker: "Brother, my sadness could fill a barrel with tears! I wish our noses were two bottles so we could pour them down one another's throats."[45] How else could that inner enemy, the intellect, be defeated?

CHAPTER 6

The Reception

F OR a moment, in 1965, Georg Büchner came to the attention of the mass media in America. The occasion was the grand opening of the Vivian Beaumont Theater in New York's Lincoln Center for the Performing Arts. The first production, considered a bad choice by much of the nation's press for a variety of reasons, was that of *Danton's Death*. It was billed as a play highly relevant to the then current political controversies in America (some felt that Robespierre was made to look like Senator Goldwater), and it came across to many of the critics representing the popular magazines as rather pointless, in any case confusing, and possibly harmful political gibberish. *Time* magazine, mirroring the attitude of a large part of the audience quite well, wrote: "Georg Buechner was an angry young German of the early 19th century . . . when he wrote the play. If he were alive today he would presumably burn his draft card and spare the drama."[1] Neither the political nor the journalistic establishment was much in the mood for receiving advice from the younger generation that year. The play seemed to communicate attitudes regarded as dangerously muddleheaded, if not altogether cowardly defeatist, in the face of what the fourth estate still considered to be the unquestionably essential mission of the war effort in Viet Nam. In the figure of Danton, the same reviewer saw "a compulsive blabbertongue who would rather rant than fight," showing perhaps a greater insight into the play than into the changing political currents of the time. For people who prefer fighting to ranting the theater is, of course, the wrong place to look for action. Nevertheless, the political message of the play—that revolution is no less futile than other human activities—even though it angered him, was understood quite well by this reviewer, as he showed when he went on to write: "The play is a petrified forest of conflicting themes. It can be variously regarded as a study in revolutionary disillusionment, an attack on revolutionary fanaticism or a defense of revolutionary intransigence." What this interpretation does not, or will not, allow for is the possibility that not only the play but the political process itself is a petrified forest of conflicting themes, and that this is at least a part of what Büchner wanted to communicate.

The fault did not lie solely with the particular, severely criticized production at the Beaumont, for neither *Danton's Death* nor *Woyzeck* has enjoyed much success on the big stages of the world. Even in Germany, where today Büchner is regarded as one of a handful of truly "great" writers, stage successes have been limited and very slow in coming. The problems have been the same everywhere. The major barriers to a wider appreciation of his work are the expectations brought into the theatre by the audiences. Those who come expecting in *Danton's Death* a typical nineteenth-century tragedy of betrayal—perhaps a later version of Friedrich Schiller's *Wallenstein's Death*—are as disappointed as those who come in the hope of hearing the romantic "fighting" words of the liberal revolutionaries. Existential "ranting," even where it is recognized and appreciated, simply does not belong in the great cultural palaces no matter how modishly subdued the decor. Critic Harold Clurman, in trying to come to grips with the ineffectiveness of the Lincoln Center performance of "so rich a play," felt the dissonance when he wrote:

My bewilderment at what was happening or not happening in this notable play . . . was so upsetting that I began to blame the very edifice in which I found myself. Perhaps, I thought, the theatre itself, a combination of imposing architectural forms, with large esplanades fronted by a gigantic Henry Moore sculpture and a square pool, with an interior which is neither exactly intimate nor epically sweeping was at fault. But that is going too far! The trouble lies elsewhere. There is some deep incongruity in the assembled elements: the text, the company, the audience (what's Hecuba to them and they to Hecuba?), the premises and the auspices of the occasion.[2]

Maybe it is not only the conspiracy of the elements assembled but also of those missing which tends to condemn Büchner's plays to failure on the electronically controlled escalating and rotating stages of the great houses. The people who want to confront such problematical texts (are they perhaps the "doubters" whom Büchner writes about as opposed to the "knowers"?) have long ago learned to shy away from such places. They are the ones who go to the little playhouses found all over America on college campuses and out in the neighborhoods, or even in abandoned wineries in Yountville, California. In these places, plays like Brecht's *Baal*, Samuel Beckett's *Waiting for Godot*, Tennessee Williams *El Camino Real*, Eugène Ionesco's *The Chairs*, and Peter Handke's *Kaspar* play to often half-empty houses and are nevertheless successes. Here too, among such spiritual descendants, Büchner's dramas find their real home. Even *Leonce and Lena*, nowadays sometimes presented under the rubric "theater of the absurd," is given an occasional trial.

Büchner's "success" on this level of theater has to do with the fact that he touches upon the main currents of twentieth-century thought in an idiom that has come to dominate the literature of the last fifty years. Except in the German-speaking countries, his following is still very limited, but in those circles where he is known he has long been recognized as one of the wellsprings of the modern theater. Playwright Jack Richardson, also commenting on the 1965 Beaumont performance, though he too found the active, revolutionary side of *Danton's Death* inadequately developed, nevertheless reminded his readers of the debt owed its author in these terms:

Sartre, Camus, Malraux, Silone, as well as lesser writers have made themselves the heirs to these problems (as explored in *Danton*), and in a raw century, when every secret of mankind seems to have been uprooted and exposed, they have perhaps offered us more subtle analyses of them. But it was Büchner who sounded the major chord for these works, and we have lived, unbeknownst to so many, within his strange harmony ever since. No less remarkable than the young dramatist's insights into history is the language he expressed them with. . . . Indeed if there is such a thing as modern dramatic rhetoric, then Büchner, in *Danton's Death* and *Woyzeck*, created it.[3]

It is not really possible to tell the extent of Büchner's direct influence upon his heirs, who are, of course, not just the French and Italian writers mentioned by Richardson, but can be found everywhere. Büchner did not somehow invent the ideas which became the orthodoxies of many of the leading intellectuals of another century. Rather, Büchner looked at the world with much the same unsentimental, uncompromising severity which became characteristic of the intellectual community after Darwin, Nietzsche, and Freud. Human problems have changed but little in the one hundred and fifty years since Johann Woyzeck mounted the scaffold; what has changed is the way of looking at them. Even without Büchner these problems would have been seen in a new light by the probing eyes of later generations: by the eyes of the naturalists, the impressionists, the expressionists, of the existentialists, the structuralists, the ecologists, to name some of the obvious inheritors of his somewhat poisonous legacy. The specific contributions he made to the fabric of modern thought, considerable though they are, can hardly be sifted out. Not only the literature of the last seventy years, but also certain current directions in the behavioral sciences reflect and, what is perhaps more important, serve to make Büchner's intuitive psychological ideas seem very modern indeed. They turn up in many different places. For example, his conceptions about madness and sanity are strikingly consistent with such influential recent works as Michel Foucault's history of madness (English title: *Madness and Civilization*, 1965). Not only theoreticians but also experimental psychologists, though they are still somewhat ill-at-ease because such ideas are viewed with great suspicion especially by many of their clinical colleagues, are ever more boldly raising the Büchneresque question: "If sanity and insanity exist, how shall we know them?" Psychologist D. L. Rosenhan, in an article entitled "On Being Sane in Insane Places,"[4] poses precisely this question and then describes an experiment that offers considerable "scientific" corroboration for the conclusion that the distinction between sane and insane behavior is anything but clear.[5] Rosenhan's careful, almost apologetic language suggests a feeling, on his part, that such ideas are not much less radical today than they were in Büchner's day:

To raise questions regarding normality and abnormality is in no way to question the fact that some behaviors are deviant and odd. Murder is deviant. So, too, are hallucinations. Nor does raising such questions deny the existence of personal anguish that is often associated with "mental illness." . . . But normality and abnormality, sanity and insanity, and the diagnoses that flow from them may be less substantive than many believe them to be.[6]

[130]

Indeed, Büchner, who was not restricted by the necessity for either scientific objectivity or scientific dogmatism, went much further in his *Woyzeck*. He goes on to ask, in effect, whether even murder and hallucination are actually "deviant," or if they do not also represent "normal" responses to the human condition. This question, posed so long ago in literary terms, seems just now to be looming on the horizon of scientific discovery.

Büchner's strictly literary influences are somewhat more specifically discernible than his intellectual contributions, simply because the field is more limited. It was just about ten years after his rediscovery in 1879 that the German naturalistic theater began a very rapid development encouraged by the opening of the "Freie Bühne" (Free Stage) in Berlin which offered the new, at that time highly controversial, plays performance opportunities. Foremost among the naturalistic dramatists was Gerhart Hauptmann, who, beginning with *Vor Sonnenaufgang* (Before Dawn, 1889), delivered a series of formidable plays at a rate of one a year over the next fifteen years, before turning with markedly less success toward symbolism. During this early period, Büchner's influence upon him was profound. Outstanding among these works is *The Weavers*, which explores the plight of the poor with the same dismayed objectivity previously found only in *Woyzeck*. Although it is a sociopolitical play built upon the theme of poverty and lacks the existential dimension, Hauptmann, like Büchner, has no solutions, no advice, but only bitter tears to offer to the innocent victims of a cruel reality. Even more explicit than Büchner about the role of the church in adding to the burdens of the poor while tickling the vanity of the rich, the play gravitates toward a nihilistic conclusion. Driven by the absolute hopelessness of their situation, the weavers, having been displaced from their trade by the machines, rise up in a final, pointless orgy of violence to plunder, smash, kill and, ultimately, to be killed themselves. Like Büchner, Hauptmann followed the historical sources closely and used the language of the people. A somewhat different relationship to Büchner can be felt in Hauptmann's dream play *Hannele,* where the tragedy involves the sharp contrast between a barren and ugly reality and the majesty of childish dreams. Sunday-school conceptions of paradise mix in the dreams of a young girl with the impressions of an awakening sexuality, composed largely of fairy-tale elements causing her to forsake a cruel existence for death. Hauptmann's technique of flashing back and forth between reality and dreams, which are actually represented on the stage—a technique he used again somewhat less effectively in *The Sunken Bell*—is strongly reminiscent of Büchner's fractured scene structure. But the most important connection between the two writers is in the introduction of the language of the poor into the literary tragedy, thereby opening the way to the social desegregation of the stage in the new century.

A different kind of relationship to Büchner can be found in Hauptmann's Viennese contemporary Artur Schnitzler. Appreciated today chiefly for his absurdist drama *The Green Cockatoo* (1899), and the melancholy sex play *La Ronde*, Schnitzler concerned himself primarily with the demythologization of the traditional literary concepts of love and death. Though his ideas closely parallel Büchner's use of these themes, particularly in *Leonce and Lena*, Schnitzler, in his plays as well as in his many narrative works, leans more specifically upon early Freudian theory. As a physician, he was trained, like Büchner, in the biological sciences which might help to explain a kind of clinically amoral tone that sometimes takes the form of very explicit sexual eroticism in both writers, though the solid earthiness found in *Danton's Death* and *Woyzeck* is not often echoed in his works. More important than the thematic similarities are the close esthetic links. Both in his narrative and his theatrical pieces, Schnitzler focuses heavily upon what might be called the artistically incisive moments in the action. Rather than aiming to achieve smooth chronological continuities, he follows Büchner's example in creating in his writings series of disconnected scenes or "pictures," as Büchner had called them in *Lenz*, which fall into contrasting rather than supportive patterns.

Moving along quite different paths, both the naturalists and Schnitzler's Viennese circle of writers, sometimes called the literary impressionists, brought a higher degree of Büchner's kind of realism into the theater. In some ways, Schnitzler, though he has struck many literary critics as being playful, or even frivolous, comes closer to Büchner's spirit than the people around the *Freie Bühne* in Berlin, despite their loud claim to the heritage. For the naturalists, the human tragedy lay in the collision between people and the inalterable social forces that ultimately control them. In this they follow more closely in the more traditional footsteps of Friedrich Hebbel. Schnitzler, on the other hand, locates the human problem exactly where Büchner does, i.e., in the all too readily deluded mind. On the surface, his figures seem to be playing at life. Unaware of their own illusions, they try to live out their dreams as if they were reality. *Liebelei* (The Game of Love, 1895) looks like a "game" only to the audience, but not to the participants. It is not altogether Schnitzler's fault that theater-goers do not always recognize themselves and their own illusions in the mirrors he holds up to them. They do not recognize themselves because they take their own "games" as seriously as the figures in the plays do theirs. Perhaps more gently, but no less incisively, than Büchner, Schnitzler unveils a deep and demeaning absurdity in human existence. He adopts the bitter tones of *Leonce and Lena* rather than the dark and desperate tones of *Woyzeck,* but his insight into life is therefore no less tragic.

Frank Wedekind was perhaps the most consciously devoted of the early Büchner followers. It was through him that Büchner's dramatic rhetoric entered into the mainstream of the German theater. His many plays, beginning with *Frühlings Erwachen* (The Awakening of Spring, 1891), seem dominated by Büchner's conception of man as "unideal nature." Far less tough-minded than his mentor, Wedekind seemed to harbor hopes that man could find his way back to nature through a new enlightenment and saw himself in the role of proclaimer of the new morality. His plays are populated with grotesque types built upon the pattern of the Doctor and the Captain in *Woyzeck.* With Lulu, the heroine of both *Der Erdgeist* (The Earth Spirit, 1895) and *Die Büchse der Pandora* (Pandora's Box, 1904), he created his version of the new woman who spurns social convention in favor of an instinctual re-alliance with "ideal nature." But it is finally Wedekind's use of language that makes him the most important bridge between Büchner and the moderns. Though he falls far short of Büchner's poetic power, he aims for the same effects. His characters, speaking out of their own narrow visions, fail to understand each other and talk past one another in seemingly nonsensical dialogues which nevertheless carry the author's message to the audience. Earthy, often crude language is used, perhaps more self-consciously and hence less effectively than by

Büchner, to shock the audience into an awareness of the artificiality of its own social attitudes. Though he was not adverse to rational argument and artificial manipulation of sympathies, Wedekind preferred Büchneresque confrontation tactics to the seductive stratagems of his contemporaries.

The transformation of the stage from a platform for the friendly persuasion of the audience into an instrument of confrontation is probably the most important dramaturgical development of this century. Wedekind was followed in this direction by the expressionistic playwrights, first by Carl Sternheim, and then by Georg Kaiser and Ernst Toller. Through them, the chaos of a world gone mad was hurled at an audience in the mood to be insulted rather than amused. Surrounding the First World War, there was an atmosphere that generated a hunger for the kind of tough vision represented by Büchner. It was a period of new editions of his works, Landau's in 1909, Franz's in 1912, Hausenstein's in 1916, Witkowski's in 1920, Bergemann's (which with its subsequent revisions served over two generations as the "critical edition") in 1922, and Arnold Zweig's in 1923. In 1921, confrontation tactics penetrated even the most conservative of all the cultural bastions of our time: the opera house. The wedge was Alban Berg's musical masterwork *Wozzeck*, an opera based on the text of Büchner's *Woyzeck*.[7] Although Berg emasculated the play by removing "offensive" passages such as the carnival scenes, thereby blurring the existential focus of the play, the score, in its relentless atonal intensity, does represent a fitting musical counterpart to Büchner's tightly structured image of chaos. A much later attempt by the Swiss composer Gottfried von Einem to bring *Danton's Death* (1947) into the plush setting of the operatic stage has met with far more limited success.

The major theoretician and practitioner of the new threatrical forms between the two wars was Bertolt Brecht. With his antidramatic concept of the "epic theater," he sought to give critical definition to the spirit of audience confrontation. As a writer of plays, he was the first since Büchner to master the art of molding the common everyday speech of ordinary people into powerful poetic images. The reflection of Büchner's language is particularly strong in his earliest plays, like *Baal* (1922) and *A Man's a Man*. The scene structure, too, points to a close relationship, but Brecht was no imitator and quickly developed his own idiom. He saw in Büchner a fellow revolutionary against the German classical dramatic tradition, and he assigned himself the task of continuing that revolution. But his conception of the theater as an educational institution for the betterment of society is totally alien to Büchner. Despite the chaos reflected in his plays, Brecht saw the human problem as stemming from corrigible moral weaknesses, such as greed and the lust for power. Nevertheless, his plays often reveal a close kinship to Büchner's themes. Particularly during the period of his exile in the late thirties and early forties, Brechtian "heroes" such as Mother Courage and Galileo strongly reflect Danton's seemingly wishy-washy combination of toughness and "cowardliness." In *Herr Puntila und Sein Knecht Matti*, Brecht explores the beneficial effects of alcoholic intoxication in the same half-serious and half-frivolous tone in which Büchner approaches the theme in *Woyzeck*. The revolutionary people's judge, Azdak, in the *Caucasian Chalk Circle*, who knows nothing about the law and therefore much about justice, seems to be cut from the same cloth as some of the officials of the little kingdoms of Pipi and Popo in *Leonce and ʟena*. Many more specific points of contact could be cited, yet Brecht does not follow Büchner to the edge of the abyss. Though there is desperation in his work, there is also hope and a somewhat shaky faith in the possibility of political solutions.

The nihilistic side of Büchner found more fertile soil in France—first among the existentialists and, after the Second World War, among the creators of the "theater of the absurd," where his techniques as well as his conception of life took root. Here the desperate isolation and uselessness of the human condition is explored over and over again. Of course, the comic element is more heavily pronounced than in *Danton's Death* or in *Woyzeck*, but it is grotesque comedy, full of tragic overtones. It would be hard to find a more apt description of the types that populate plays like Eugène Ionesco's *The Bald Soprano* and Samuel Beckett's *Waiting for Godot* than Leonce's characterization of mankind:

What people won't do out of mere boredom! They study out of boredom, pray out of boredom, they love, they marry and multiply out of boredom, and—what makes it so amusing—they do it with the most serious of countenances, without ever understanding why, and God knows what else. These heroes, these geniuses, these simpletons, these saints, these sinners, these fathers of families, are, after all, nothing more than refined indolent idlers.[8]

Ionesco's *The Lesson* (1951), a play about a ludicrous language teacher who, in the end, stabs and mutilates his bored pupil is more than incidentally related to Büchner. The murder scene is a gruesome parody of the one in *Woyzeck*, and the "Professor" himself is a modern reconstruction of the Doctor. Just as Büchner had based the substance of the Doctor's simplistic dogmatism upon his own field of study, medicine, so Ionesco, a former language teacher, made his Mr. Know-it-all into a linguist whose ridiculous theories reveal the pointlessness of his endeavor:

That which distinguishes the neo-Spanish languages from each other and their idioms from other linguistic groups, such as the groups of languages called Austrian, and neo-Austrian or Hapsburgian, as well as the Esperanto, Helvetian, Monacan, Swiss, Andorran, Basque and jai alai groups, and also the groups of diplomatic and technical languages—that which distinguishes them, I repeat, is their striking resemblance which makes it so hard to distinguish them from each other. . . .[9]

As Leonce had said, the amusing part is in the serious countenances of such people as the Professor, but there is tragedy in the comic revelation: "Why must *I* be the one to know this," the Prince of Popo had asked himself. That the world is absurd is not in itself tragic; it is the capacity to recognize the absurdity that robs man of his dream of an orderly world.

In the 1950's and 1960's, Büchner's "types" started to appear in plays throughout the world. This is partly due to the enormous influence exerted by Brecht on the one hand, and the French absurdists on the other, but Büchner himself now began to be more widely known on the international scene. From the Brazilian black revolutionary playwright Abdias do Nascimento to the Polish absurdist Slawomir Mrozek the echoes can be heard. A whole series of Büchneresque formulations come together in a single bit of dialogue in Mrozek's *Tango* (1965):

ARTHUR: I was insane! There's no going back, no present, no future. There's nothing.

[*136*]

The Reception

STOMIL (*evading him*): What is he now? A nihilist?
ALA (*tearing off her veil*): What about me? Am I nothing? . . . You're
a coward, that's all you are. A child and a coward and impotent!
ARTHUR: No please don't say that. I'm not afraid, but I can't believe
anymore. I'll do anything. I'll lay down my life . . . but there's no
turning back to the old forms. They can't create a reality for us. I was
wrong.
ALA: What are you talking about?
ARTHUR: About creating a world. . . .
EUGENE: . . . You're drunk. You don't know what you're saying.
ARTHUR: Yes, drunk. When I was sober I let myself be deceived, so
I got drunk to dispel my illusions. You'd better have a drink too,
Uncle.[10]

All the symptoms of the human tragedy as Büchner had seen it
are unveiled here. Arthur awakens from the "insanity" that had
given substance to his life. His hopes and beliefs crumble into
dust. Mrozek even relates sexual impotence to the awakening,
and his conception of alcohol as the medication needed to face
a world without self-deception seems to derive straight from
Woyzeck.

In one important respect, however, the modern theatrical
tradition has moved in a direction opposite to Büchner's. Along
with the other art media, the theater has become progressively
more abstract. The trend was hastened by Brecht's theories which
banished the illusion of reality from the theater. In order to avoid
educationally counterproductive sympathetic attachments, so
went his thinking, the audience must at all times be made aware
that it is sitting in the theater watching actors perform, rather
than witnessing real events unfurl before its eyes. This argument
surely hits Büchner as hard as it does the naturalists at whom it
was aimed; for historical accuracy and the illusion of reality were
his most vital esthetic concerns. Though Büchner's message was
very similar to Ionesco's, he did not turn man into a rhinoceros
in order to demonstrate his absurdity. He sought to demonstrate
the freakishness of man by trying to reproduce, as faithfully as
possible, the gestures and words of real people.

Only recently the movement toward ever greater abstraction,
which on the German stage flowed from Brecht to the Swiss
writers Friedrich Dürrenmatt and Max Frisch, and from there
to the plays of Günter Grass and Peter Handke, has met with

some resistance from the so-called "documentary" plays of Peter Weiss. After his *Marat/de Sade* (1964), a play so intimately related to *Danton's Death* that it is difficult to think of one without recalling the other, Weiss in his *Investigation* (1965) carried Büchner's concern for historical accuracy to its ultimate limit by "distilling" the dialogue out of the records and newspaper accounts of the Auschwitz trials at Frankfurt in 1963–65.[11] But Weiss, a committed political writer, clinging to the belief that social reorganization can solve human problems, fills his works with the kind of political rhetoric that might even satisfy the fighting spirit of the critic from *Time* magazine who was so offended by Danton's "blabbertongue." *Trotzki in Exile* (1971), too, is a heavily documented play; Weiss even includes a bibliography of his sources. It might well be regarded the *Danton's Death* of the Russian Revolution. There are many striking similarities, particularly in the discussions among the revolutionary functionaries, their camaraderie as well as the conflicts between them. But if there is merit to Jack Richardson's idea that Büchner developed the human side of Danton well but not the revolutionary in him, then the reverse might be said of Trotzki in Weiss's play.

Notes and References

Chapter One

1. Büchner's brother Ludwig published a selection of the works and letters at Frankfurt a.M. in 1850. The edition which brought Büchner to the attention of the general public, however, was the one prepared by Karl Emil Franzos (Frankfurt a.M., 1879).

2. Georg Büchner, *Sämtliche Werke und Briefe*, ed. W. R. Lehmann (Hamburg, 1967 ff.; vols. III & IV announced, but not yet available), II, p. 25 ff. This edition will henceforth be cited as *Lehmann*.

3. Georg Büchner, *Werke und Briefe*, ed. F. Bergemann (Wiesbaden, 1958), p. 552. This edition will henceforth be cited as *Bergemann*. Unless otherwise indicated, translations are my own.

4. See Bergemann, p. 552 ff.

5. See Karl Viëtor, *Georg Büchner* (Berne, 1949), pp. 23–27.

6. Lehmann, II, p. 416.

7. Bergemann, p. 559.

8. Lehmann, II, p. 426.

9. Lehmann, II, p. 423.

10. Bergemann, p. 559 ff.

11. Lehmann, II, p. 425.

12. For biographical sketches of Büchner's fellow conspirators, see Viëtor, op. cit., p. 43 ff.

13. Carl R. Mueller's English translation does not indicate Weidig's emendations but omits his additions. See Georg Büchner, *Complete Plays and Prose* (New York, 1963), p. 169 ff. This edition will henceforth be cited as *Mueller*.

14. There is evidence that the society was betrayed by Konrad Kuhl, an associate of Weidig. See Viëtor, op. cit., p. 79 ff.

15. It is possible that Clemm also betrayed the society and was directly responsible for Becker's arrest. In any case, Büchner thought so: see Lehmann, II, p. 441.

16. According to Büchner's brother, Wilhelm; see Bergemann, p. 567.

17. Lehmann, II, p. 475.

18. *Ibid.*

19. Lehmann, II, p. 436.
20. Cf. Bergemann, p. 616.
21. See Lehmann, II, p. 464.
22. See Lehmann, II, p. 291 ff.
23. A report on Büchner as a teacher was made by one of his students forty-one years later. See Bergemann, p. 571.
24. See Büchner's letter to Johann Jakob Hess, Mayor of Zurich, Lehmann, II, p. 460 f.
25. Lehmann, II, p. 455.
26. Caroline Schulz' extraordinary account of Büchner's last days deserves mention as a literary achievement in its own right. See Bergemann, p. 575 ff.
27. Bergemann, p. 580.
28. Bergemann, p. 581.
29. Bergemann, p. 585.
30. According to Caroline Schulz, the diary was read in the presence of Wilhelmine shortly after Büchner died. It would seem reasonable that Wilhelmine kept it as a memento. See Bergemann, p. 582.
31. Bergemann, p. 582.

Chapter Two

1. I.e., Fritz König, Georg Büchner's "Danton" (Halle, 1924).
2. Mueller, p. 169.
3. The classic interpretation of Danton along these lines is Viëtor, op. cit., p. 95 ff. Also falling into this category are those analyses which see Danton primarily as a document of nihilism, i.e., Benno von Wiese, Die deutsche Tragödie von Lessing bis Hebbel (Hamburg, 1948), II, p. 325 ff.
4. The most radical Marxist interpretation is that by Georg Lukács, who denounces the interpretations in the Viëtor tradition as fascist. Viëtor himself does not escape the fascist label—a fact which must strike those who know Viëtor and his works as amusing. See "Der faschistisch verfälschte und der wirkliche George Büchner," in Lukács, Deutsche Realisten des 19. Jahrhunderts (Berlin, 1952), p. 66 ff. Hans Mayer provides the most elegant and convincing version of this kind of interpretation in Georg Büchner und seine Zeit (Wiesbaden, 1960), p. 182 ff.
5. These interpretations move in diverse directions. Some of the most important ones are: Gerhart Baumann, Georg Büchner: Die dramatische Ausdruckswelt (Göttingen, 1961), p. 9 ff.; Walter Höllerer, "Dantons Tod," Das deutsche Drama vom Barock zur Gegenwart, ed. Benno von Wiese (Düsseldorf, 1962), II, p. 62 ff.; and in English, Herbert Lindenberger, Georg Büchner (Carbondale, 1964), p. 19 ff.

6. For a thorough analysis of the dramatic structure in Büchner, see Helmut Krapp, *Der Dialog bei Georg Büchner* (Darmstadt, 1958).

7. For a thorough treatment of Büchner's sources for *Danton* see Viëtor, "Die Quellen zu Büchners Drama 'Dantons Tod,'" *Euphorion* 34 (1933), pp. 357–379.

8. See the reprint of the original ed. of 1835: Büchner, *Dantons Tod* (Zürich, 1947), p. iii. For Büchner's negative response to the subtitle, see Lehmann, II, p. 443.

9. Lehmann, II, p. 443.

10. Lehmann, I, p. 9. For the purpose of close analysis, I prefer my own, more literal translation here to Mueller's which, though it captures the spirit of the passage, is quite free.

11. *Hamlet*, III, 2, l. 126.

12. Lehmann, I, p. 19. Cf. Mueller, p. 13.

13. The words: "The statue of liberty has not yet been cast," certainly mean that not even the idea of freedom has taken shape. The strong emphasis placed on them by the label "prophecy" precludes the interpretation that liberty is not yet a reality, which would simply be a statement of the obvious.

14. Lehmann, I, p. 12 ff.; Mueller, p. 6 ff.

15. Mueller, p. 12 f.; Lehmann, I, p. 18.

16. Mueller, p. 9; Lehmann, I, p. 15.

17. *Ibid.*

18. "You are a powerful echo," Mueller, p. 27; Lehmann, I, p. 32.

19. Lehmann, I, p. 11. Cf. Mueller, p. 5 f.

20. Mueller, p. 15; Lehmann, I, p. 20 f.

21. Mueller, p. 17; Lehmann, I, p. 22.

22. Lehmann, I, p. 26. Mueller's translation: "My God, the time we've lost! But it was worth every minute!" (p. 20), contains a tone of regret not found in the German, "So viel Zeit zu verlieren! Das war der Mühe wert!" The idea that Danton regrets not having spent this time at more important endeavors does not fit into the context of the drama.

23. Lehmann, I, p. 28. Cf. Mueller, p. 22.

24. Mueller, p. 22; Lehmann, I, p. 27.

25. Mueller, p. 21; Lehmann, I, p. 26.

26. Mueller, p. 21; Lehmann, I, p. 26.

27. Mueller, p. 23; Lehmann, I, p. 28.

28. Mueller, p. 25; Lehmann, I, p. 30.

29. Mueller, p. 40; Lehmann, I, p. 45.

30. I have changed Mueller's translation slightly in order to preserve Büchner's term *idée fixe*, which he uses elsewhere in an obviously technical sense. Cf. Mueller, p. 65 f.; Lehmann, I, p. 70.

31. Mueller, p. 42; Lehmann, I, p. 47.
32. Mueller, p. 56; Lehmann, I, p. 61.
33. See Mueller, p. 48 ff.; Lehmann, I, p. 52 ff.
34. Mueller, p. 57; Lehmann, I, p. 61.
35. *Ibid.*
36. Mueller, p. 62; Lehmann, I, p. 66.

Chapter Three

1. *Der Dichter Lenz und Friedericke von Sesenheim* (Basel, 1842). In a footnote, he refers to his essay as the basis of Büchner's "unfortunately fragmentary novella *Lenz.*" See Bergemann, p. 589.
2. J. M. R. Lenz, *Gesammelte Schriften,* ed. Ludwig Tieck (Berlin, 1828), 3 vols.
3. *Poetry and Truth,* Book XIV, from the beginning.
4. Literary criticism has always dwelled on Lenz's "aping" of Goethe. Even his unsuccessful courtship of Friederike Brion, whose love Goethe had previously won and betrayed, is interpreted as a psychotic following in Goethe's footsteps. Tradition has probably led to exaggerations. My own conclusions about the Goethe-Lenz relationship, based largely upon Lenz's letters and Goethe's letters and memoirs, are that Lenz failed to notice that his warm friendship for Goethe, albeit somewhat tinctured by envy, was never returned with equal enthusiasm, forcing Goethe into attempts to shake him off, which, in turn, led to outbursts of jealousy on Lenz's part. In any case, Goethe's coldness toward Lenz clearly expresses itself in the passage from *Poetry and Truth,* where he remembers him chiefly as a lover of intrigue and a victim "of the spirit of the time which should have come to an end through the appearance of *Werther.*"
5. Lehmann, II, p. 423.
6. Lehmann, II, p. 428. Cf. J. M. R. Lenz, *Gesammelte Schriften,* ed. Franz Blei (Munich and Leipzig, 1909), I, p. 134 ff.
7. In order to come as close as possible to the German stylistic peculiarities, I did not use the much smoother translation in Mueller (p. 145) here. See Lehmann, I, p. 82.
8. Mueller, p. 147; Lehmann, I, p. 84.
9. Mueller, p. 149; Lehmann, I, p. 86.
10. Lehmann, II, p. 291 ff., esp. p. 292 f. Büchner's ideas about what he calls the "philosophical" approach to biology largely reflect Goethe's, in whose footsteps he launches the attack upon teleology. In the essay, Büchner cites Goethe's *Metamorphosis of the Plant* for its pioneering spirit (p. 352).
11. Mueller, p. 152; Lehmann, I, p. 88.
12. See Lehmann, II, p. 443 f.

13. Mueller, p. 149 f.; Lehmann, I, p. 86.

14. Although Büchner actually applies this definition only to the "dramatic poet," the text of *Lenz*, which otherwise follows Oberlin's account exceptionally closely, would seem to justify including the narrative poet. Lehmann, II, p. 443.

15. Although *Lenz* cannot be considered a completed work because of an obvious gap in the text (Mueller, p. 165; Lehmann, I, p. 100), there can be little doubt that this sentence was to mark the end of the work, for the passage immediately preceding it corresponds perfectly to the end of Oberlin's account (see Lehmann, I, p. 482 f.).

16. Lindenberger, op. cit., p. 71. The parenthesis is Lindenberger's.

17. To preserve certain stylistic peculiarities, I have used my own translation here: Lehmann, I, p. 79. Cf. Mueller, p. 141.

18. Mueller, p. 143. In the last sentence I changed the translation of Büchner's "es ward ihm leicht." Mueller's "He felt better" catches the simple tone of the German more successfully. Unfortunately, the word "felt" affects the progression of perspectives. Since preserving this progression is my prime concern here, I prefer the more laborious "his spirit was lightened." Lehmann, I, p. 80.

19. Mueller, p. 143 f.; Lehmann, I, p. 81.

20. Mueller, p. 158; Lehmann, I, p. 93 f.

21. Mueller, p. 145; Lehmann, I, p. 82.

22. Mueller, p. 160; Lehmann, I, 95 f.

23. Mueller, p. 76; Lehmann, I, p. 106. Similar ideas also find expression in both *Danton* and *Woyzeck*.

Chapter Four

1. The substance of this chapter has been published previously in *Monatshefte*, LIII (1961), 338 ff.

2. See Bergemann, p. 612 f.

3. Karl Viëtor, *Georg Büchner* (Berne, 1949), pp. 174–188. A. H. J. Knight, *Georg Büchner* (Oxford, 1951), pp. 92–112. Herbert Lindenberger, *Georg Büchner* (Carbondale, 1964), pp. 54–67. Friedrich Gundolf, "Georg Büchner," *Zeitschrift für Deutschkunde*, 43 (1929), 9–10.

4. Cf. Knight, op. cit., p. 93.

5. Lehmann, II, p. 444.

6. Mueller, p. 133; Lehmann, I, p. 427.

7. Op. cit., p. 188.

8. Mueller, p. 105; Lehmann, I, p. 134.

9. See Lindenberger, op. cit., p. 57.

10. Mueller, p. 75 f.; Lehmann, I, 105.

11. See above: Note 22, Chapter 3.

12. Mueller, p. 65 f.; Lehmann, p. 69 ff.

13. Mueller, p. 77; Lehmann, p. 107.
14. Mueller, p. 78; Lehmann, I, p. 108.
15. Mueller, p. 83; Lehmann, I, p. 112.
16. According to Lacroix. See Mueller, p. 15; Lehmann, I, p. 20 f.
17. Mueller, p. 82; Lehmann, I, p. 112.
18. Mueller, p. 87; Lehmann, I, p. 116.
19. Mueller, p. 94; Lehmann, I, p. 123.
20. See Mueller, p. 144; Lehmann, I, p. 81.
21. My translation from Lehmann, p. 118. Cf. Mueller, p. 89.
22. Mueller, p. 90; Lehmann, I, p. 119.
23. Mueller, p. 95; Lehmann, I, p. 124 f.
24. "Sehnsucht nach dem Tode," *Hymnen an die Nacht*, Athenäums-Fassung #6.
25. Mueller, p. 101 f.; Lehmann, I, p. 131.
26. Mueller, p. 104 f.; Lehmann, I, p. 133.
27. Mueller, p. 94; Lehmann, I, p. 123.
28. Goethe, *The Sorrows of Young Werther*, transl. by Hutter (New York, 1962), p. 97.
29. *Ibid.*

Chapter Five

1. For the complex history of the editorial development of the text of *Woyzeck* and the problems relating to the manuscripts see Lehmann, *Büchner: Textkritische Noten* (Hamburg, 1967), pp. 35–66. Although there is some evidence that Büchner finished the play, this fact cannot be absolutely established. In any case, no definitive manuscript has been found. The various published editions are based on four separate, partially overlapping, fragmentary drafts. These are printed in raw form for the first time in Lehmann, I, pp. 143–181. In the same volume, pp. 337–406, there is a "Synopsis" of the play. The various fragments are printed side by side where they overlap. A new "Reading and Stage Text" follows on pp. 407–431. Certain problems of scene sequences and wording have not been resolved, nor are they likely to be resolved. Equally uncertain is the question of the ending of the play. Did Büchner intend to bring Woyzeck to trial, or did Woyzeck die by his own hand after the murder? Modern criticism leans toward the latter view, especially since Wolfgang Marten's "Der Barbier in Büchners 'Woyzeck,'" *Zeitschrift für deutsche Philologie*, LXXIX (1960), 361–383.

2. My account of the case is based on the two reports by J. C. Clarus, "Die Zurechnungsfähigkeit des Mörders Johann Christian Woyzeck, nach Grundsätzen der Staatsarzneikunde Aktenmässig erwiesen" and "Früheres Gutachten des Herrn Hofrat Dr. Clarus über den Gemüthszustand des Mörders Joh. Christ. Woyzeck, erstattet am

Notes and References

16. Sept. 1821." The former of these reports was published in several places. Both originally appeared in separate issues of the *Zeitschrift für Staatsarzneikunde* (Leipzig), the first in 1824, the other in 1826. Büchner must have found them there since his play contains unmistakable elements from both. They are reprinted in Lehmann, I, pp. 485–549.

3. Lehmann, I, p. 547.

4. Lehmann, I, p. 525 f.

5. Lehmann, I, p. 534.

6. Hans Mayer, *Georg Büchner und seine Zeit* (Wiesbaden, 1960), p. 331.

7. Mueller, p. 36; Bergemann, p. 45; Lehmann, I, p. 41.

8. Hans Mayer, op. cit., p. 331 f.

9. Herbert Lindenberger, *Georg Büchner* (Carbondale, 1964), p. 107.

10. A. H. J. Knight, *Georg Büchner* (Oxford, 1951), p. 131.

11. Karl Viëtor, "Woyzeck," in *Georg Büchner*, ed. Wolfgang Martens (Darmstadt, 1965), p. 173.

12. Lehmann, I, p. 490.

13. Lehmann, I, p. 546.

14. Lehmann, II, p. 426.

15. The passage is quoted above, p. 26. See also note 9, Chapter 2, above.

16. Knight, op. cit., p. 131.

17. Mueller, p. xxiv. Mueller's brief introductory remarks to *Woyzeck* are highly perceptive in other ways as well.

18. See Lehmann, I, p. 496, also p. 508 f.

19. Lehmann, I, p. 506.

20. Such attacks are cited by Henke, the publisher of the *Zeitschrift für Staatsarzneikunde*, who defends Clarus against them. See Lehmann, I, p. 538 f.

21. Mueller, p. 109; Bergemann, p. 151; Lehmann, I, p. 414. Since Mueller used Bergemann's edition for his translation, and since there are some basic differences between Bergemann and Lehmann in this play, references to both will be cited here.

22. Mueller, p. 83; Bergemann, p. 123; Lehmann, I. p. 112.

23. E.g. Viëtor, "Woyzeck," op. cit., p. 157 f. Despite the fact that Viëtor draws a parallel between the Captain and King Peter in *Leonce and Lena*, he still sees the Captain primarily as the spokesman for the moral attitudes of the old, solid middle class.

24. The theory that "Street. Captain-Doctor" was intended by Büchner as the opening scene is not unattractive. See Lehmann, "Prolegomena zu einer kritischen Büchner-Ausgabe," *Festschrift für Christian Wegner* (Hamburg, 1963), p. 190 f.

25. Mueller, p. 119; Bergemann, p. 161; Lehmann, p. 418.

26. There is a translation problem with the insults the Doctor and the Captain fling at each other. The difficulty is created by the fact that gestures as well as words are involved. Here is a literal translation of the exchange:

DOCTOR: [*Holds out his hat.*] What is that, Herr Captain? That is Hollowhead!

CAPTAIN: [*Makes a wrinkle.*] What is that, Herr Doctor? That is Onefold (*Einfalt,* which in German has the double meaning *simpleness*).

Various translators have suggested different gestures to try to rescue the very important double meaning in the Captain's response. I like Michael Hamburger's best:

CAPTAIN: [*Shows him a pin.*] And what's that, doctor? That's a nitwit. . . .

Georg Büchner, *Leonce and Lena, Lenz, Woyzeck* (Chicago & London, 1972), p. 74. Mueller's attempt leaves the issue somewhat vague:

CAPTAIN: [*makes a series of folds on his sleeve.*] And do you know who this is, Doctor? This is Sir Manifold. . . .

Mueller, p. 120.

27. The Grandmother's tale from *Woyzeck* is quoted above, p. 76. See Mueller, p. 133.

28. I have changed Mueller's translation of one sentence slightly to bring it into closer conformity with the German text. In Mueller the sentence reads: "Did I or did I not prove *to you* that the musculus . . . is controlled by *your* will." See p. 117. Bergemann, p. 158; Lehmann, I, p. 417.

29. As anyone who knows dogs well will realize, man's intellectual superiority over this animal, to which the Doctor so contemptuously compares Woyzeck, is not so very great in the specific context under discussion.

30. Mueller, p. 128; Bergemann, p. 167 f.; Lehmann, I, p. 426.

31. Another indication of the fundamental significance of this theme is the fact that in the oldest known manuscript fragment of the play, preliminary versions of the two carnival scenes are found at the very beginning. See Lehmann, I, p. 145 f.

32. Mueller, p. 114; Bergemann, p. 155; Lehmann, I, p. 411.

33. Mueller, p. 115; Bergemann, p. 156 f.; Lehmann, I, p. 412.

34. The italicized portion is my own translation. That part was left out of the Mueller translation, undoubtedly through inadvertence, p. 125. Bergemann, p. 166; Lehmann, I, p. 422.

35. Mueller, p. 110; Bergemann, p. 153; Lehmann, I, p. 415.

36. Mueller, p. 118; Bergemann, p. 159; Lehmann, I, p. 417.

37. Mueller, p. 113; Bergemann, p. 155; Lehmann, I, p. 410.

38. Mueller, p. 123; Bergemann, p. 164; Lehmann, I, p. 421.
39. Mueller, p. 116; Bergemann, p. 158; Lehmann, I, p. 413.
40. Mueller, p. 123; Bergemann, p. 164. Lehmann, in constructing his reading and stage text, in agreement with his editorial principle of using only the last known versions of the individual scenes, gives the briefer rendition of this scene as it appears in the latest draft (s. I, p. 416), thereby completely omitting the last exchange of an earlier version which contains the quoted passage. For this earlier version, see Lehmann I, p. 164 f. Especially since Büchner left space at the bottom of the ms. page in question (s. I, p. 366), there is no persuasive reason to surmise that he intended to drop the substance of the passage omitted, though he may well have wanted to reword it.
41. E.g. Knight, op. cit., p. 127 f., and Lindenberger op. cit., p. 103.
42. Mueller, p. 117; Bergemann, p. 158; Lehmann, I, p. 413.
43. Mueller, p. 130 f.; Bergemann, p. 169; Lehmann, I, p. 423.
44. Mueller includes some materials from early manuscript sources which show Woyzeck himself in a drunken stupor. Both that part of scene XII after the long speech of the First Apprentice (p. 125) and all of scene XVI (p. 129 f.) were based on several early scenes all of which were omitted by Büchner in his later draft. Part of scene XVI is based on material spoken by a figure identified as BARBER (see Lehmann, I, p. 148 f.). Wolfgang Martens, in his "Der Barbier in Büchners 'Woyzeck,'" (ed. cit., note 1, above) theorizes that this barber is a person other than Woyzeck. This theory is not completely convincing since at least some of the "Barber's" words seem to make very little sense unless they are spoken by Woyzeck. In any case, Büchner did avoid this scene as well as all other references to Woyzeck's drunkenness in his later draft.
45. Mueller, p. 124; Bergemann, p. 165; Lehmann, I, p. 421.

Chapter Six

1. *Time* (Oct. 29, 1965), p. 84.
2. *The Nation* (Nov. 16, 1965), p. 371.
3. *Commentary* (Jan., 1966), p. 56.
4. *Science* (Jan. 19, 1973), pp. 250 ff.
5. The experiment involved eight "sane" people who gained secret admission to twelve different mental hospitals by claiming to hear voices. Once admitted, these pseudo-patients stopped feigning any symptoms of abnormality. Despite their public "show" of sanity, Rosenhan points out, their sanity, though sometimes recognized by other patients, was not detected by the staff. In fact, their normal behavior patterns were usually interpreted by their warders as symptomatic of the same mental disorders diagnosed when they first arrived.

6. P. 250 f. The quotation marks around the words "mental illness" give this statement special significance. Do they signify a far more penetrating private reassessment than the language suggests?

7. The spelling *"Wozzeck"* goes back to Franzos' 1879 edition of Büchner's works. It results from Franzos' difficulty with Büchner's handwriting.

8. Mueller, p. 76; Lehmann, I, p. 106.

9. Ionesco, *Four Plays*, transl. by D. M. Allen (New York, 1958), p. 61.

10. Mrozek, *Tango*, transl. by R. Mannheim and T. Dzieduscycka (New York, 1968), p. 88 f.

11. See Weiss's notes in *Ermittlung* (Frankfurt a.M., 1965), p. 7 and p. 211.

Selected Bibliography

BIBLIOGRAPHIES

SCHLICK, WERNER. *Das Georg Büchner-Schrifttum bis 1965* (Hildes heim: Georg Olms Verlagsbuchhandlung, 1968).

PRIMARY SOURCES

Major Critical Editions

Sämtliche Werke und handschriftlicher Nachlass, ed. KARL EMIL FRANZOS. Frankfurt a.M.: J. D. Sauerländer, 1879.
Sämtliche Werke und Briefe, ed. FRITZ BERGEMANN. Leipzig: Insel, 1922. Rev.: 1926, 1940, 1949, 1952, 1956; Wiesbaden, 1953, 1958; Frankfurt a.M., 1962.
Werke und Briefe. Munich: Deutscher Taschenbuch Verlag, 1965. (Soft-cover version of the Bergemann ed.)
Sämtliche Werke und Briefe. Historisch-kritische Ausgabe mit Kommentar, ed. WERNER R. LEHMANN. Hamburg: Christian Wegner Verlag. Vol. I, 1967; vol. II, 1971; vols. III & IV announced.

Translations

The Plays of Georg Büchner. Transl. by Geoffrey Dunlop. London: Gerald Howe, 1927. Also New York: Viking Press, 1928; I. Ravin, 1952; and London: Vision Press, 1952.
A Play in Four Acts: "Danton's Death," by Georg Büchner. Transl. by Stephen Spender and Goronwy Rees. London: Faber & Faber, 1939.
"Lenz." Trans. by Michael Hamburger. In *Mandrake* (1947), no. 5, 11–32.
"Danton's Death." Transl. by Spender and Rees. In *From the Modern Repertoire*, ed. E. R. Bentley. Denver: University of Denver Press, 1949. Ser. I, pp. 29–86.
Woyzeck. Transl. by Henry Schnitzler and Seth Ulman. *New Directions in Prose and Poetry*, no. 12. London: Peter Owen, and New York: Meridian Books, 1950.
"Danton's Death." Transl. by Spender and Rees. *Treasury of the Theatre*, ed. J. Gassner, Vol. I. New York: Simon & Schuster, 1951.

"Some Büchner Letters in Translation." Transl. by Karl W. Maurer. *German Life and Letters*, no. 1 (1954/55), 50–55.

"Lenz." Transl. by Michael Hamburger. *Partisan Review*, 22 (1955), 31–46, 135–144.

"Woyzeck." Transl. by Theodore Hoffman. *The Modern Theatre*, ed. E. R. Bentley, vol. I. Garden City, N. Y.: Doubleday, 1955.

"Danton's Death." Transl. by John Holmstrom. *The Modern Theater*, ed. E. R. Bentley, vol. V. Garden City, N. Y.: Doubleday, 1957.

Danton's Death. Transl. and adapted by James Maxwell. San Francisco: Chandler Publishing Co., 1961.

"From Georg Büchner's Letters." Transl. by Maurice Edwards. *Tulane Drama Review*, 6 (1961/62), no. 3, 132–135.

"Woyzeck" and "Leonce and Lena." Transl. by Carl R. Mueller. San Francisco: Chandler Publishing Co., 1962.

Complete Plays and Prose. Transl. by Carl R. Mueller. New York: Hill and Wang, 1963. Also London, MacGibbon & Kee, 1963.

"Danton's Death." Transl. by Theodore H. Lustig. *Classical German Drama*. New York: Bantam Books, 1963.

"Woyzeck." Transl. by John Holmstrom. *Three German Plays*. Harmondsworth, Middlesex: Penguin Books, 1963.

Woyzeck. Transl. by Henry J. Schmidt. New York: Bard Books, 1969.

The Plays of Georg Büchner. Transl. by Victor Price. London: Oxford University Press, 1971.

Leonce and Lena-Lenz-Woyzeck. Transl. by Michael Hamburger. Chicago and London: University of Chicago Press, 1972.

SECONDARY SOURCES

In German

ABUTILLE, MARIO CARLO. *Angst und Zynismus bei Georg Büchner*. Berne: A. Francke Verlag, 1969.

BAUMANN, GERHART. *Georg Büchner. Die dramatische Ausdruckswelt*. Göttingen: Vandenhoeck & Ruprecht, 1961.

BRINKMANN, DONALD. *Georg Büchner als Philosoph*. Zurich: Viernheim, 1958.

BÜTTNER, LUDWIG. *Georg Büchner, Revolutionär und Pessimist*. Nuremberg: Verlag Hans Carl, 1948.

BÜTTNER, LUDWIG. *Büchners Bild vom Menschen*. Nuremberg: Verlag Hans Carl, 1967.

DIEM, EUGEN. *Georg Büchners Leben und Werk*. Heidelberg: Meister, 1946.

EBNER, FRITZ. *Georg Büchner. Ein Genius der Jugend*. Darmstadt: Turris-Verlag, 1964.

FISCHER, HEINZ. "Ein Büchner-Fund," *Deutsche Vierteljahresschrift für*

Selected Bibliography

Literaturwissenschaft und Geistesgeschichte, 44 (1970), 577–579.

FISCHER, HEINZ. *Georg Büchner—Untersuchungen und Marginalien.* Bonn: Bouvier Verlag Herbert Grundmann, 1972.

GUNKEL, RICHARD. *Georg Büchner und der Dandysmus.* Utrecht: Kemink & Zoon, 1953.

GUTZKOW, KARL. "Georg Büchner," *Meisterwerke deutscher Literaturkritik*, ed. Hans Mayer. Berlin: Rütten & Loening, 1956. Vol. II, Pt. I, pp. 215–225.

HÖLLERER, WALTER. "Büchner. 'Dantons Tod.'" *Das Deutsche Drama vom Barock bis zur Gegenwart*, ed. Benno v. Wiese. Düsseldorf: August Bagel Verlag, 1958. II, pp. 65–88.

JOHANN, ERNST (ed.). *Büchner-Preis Reden.* Stuttgart: Reclam, 1972.

KAYSER, WOLFGANG. "'Grotesk! grotesk!'—Büchners Woyzeck." *Das Groteske. Seine Darstellung in Malerei und Dichtung.* Hamburg: Rowohlt, 1960. Pp. 70–74.

KNUDSEN, HANS. *Büchner und Grabbe.* Augsburg, Stuttgart: Dr. Filser & Co., 1921.

KRAPP, HELMUT. *Der Dialog bei Georg Büchner.* Darmstadt: Gentner, 1958.

LEHMANN, WERNER R. "Prolegomena zu einer historisch-kritischen Büchner Ausgabe." *Gratulatio. Festschrift für Christian Wegner.* Hamburg: Christian Wegner, 1963. Pp. 190–225.

LEHMANN, WERNER R. "Robespierre—'ein impotenter Mahomet?'" *Euphorion*, 57 (1963), 210–217.

LUKACS, GEORG. "Der faschistisch verfälschte und der wirkliche Georg Büchner." *Deutsche Literatur in zwei Jahrhunderten.* Neuwied a. Rh., and Berlin-Spandau: Hermann Luchterhand Verlag, 1964. Pp. 249–272.

MAJUT, RUDOLF. *Studien um Büchner.* Berlin: Emil Ebering, 1932.

MARTENS, WOLFGANG. "Der Barbier in Büchners 'Woyzeck,'" *Zeitschrift für deutsche Philologie*, 79 (1960), 361–383.

MARTENS, WOLFGANG (ed.). *Georg Büchner.* Darmstadt: Wissenschaftliche Buchgesellschaft, 1965. Collection of essays by many of the leading Büchner scholars.

MAYER, HANS. *Georg Büchner und seine Zeit.* Wiesbaden: Limes Verlag, 1946 and 1960; Berlin: Verlag Volk und Welt, 1947, and Aufbau Verlag, 1960.

MÜHLHER, ROBERT. "Georg Büchner und die Mythologie des Nihilismus." In *Dichtung der Krise.* Vienna: Verlag Herold, 1951. Pp. 97–145.

OPPEL, HORST. *Die tragische Dichtung Georg Büchners.* Stuttgart: Hempe, 1951.

PENZOLDT, GÜNTHER. *Georg Büchner.* Velber bei Hannover: Erhard Friedrich, 1965.

PFEIFFER, ARTHUR. *Georg Büchner.* Frankfurt a.M.: Vittorio Klostermann, 1934.

RICHARDS, DAVID G. "Anmerkungen zur Hamburger Büchner-Ausgabe, den 'Woyzeck' betreffend." *Euphorion,* 65 (1971), 49–57.

SCHMID, PETER. *Georg Büchner. Versuch über die tragische Existenz.* Berne: Verlag Paul Haupt, 1940.

SCHRÖDER, JÜRGEN. *Georg Büchners "Leonce und Lena."* Munich-Allach: Wilhelm Fink Verlag, 1966.

VIËTOR, KARL. *Georg Büchner als Politiker.* Berne: Verlag Paul Haupt, 1939, and A. Franke Verlag, 1950.

VIËTOR, KARL. *Georg Büchner. Politik, Dichtung, Wissenschaft.* Berne: A. Franke Verlag, 1949.

WIESE, BENNO VON. "Georg Büchner. Die Tragödie des Nihilismus." *Die Deutsche Tragödie von Lessing bis Hebbel.* Hamburg: Hoffmann & Campe, 1948, 1952, 1955, 1958, 1961. 1961 ed., pp. 513–534.

WIESE, BENNO VON. "Die Religion Büchners und Hebbels." *Zwischen Utopie und Wirklichkeit.* Düsseldorf: August Bagel Verlag, 1963.

In English

BAXANDALL, LEE. "Georg Büchner's 'Danton's Death,' " *Tulane Drama Review,* 6 (1961/62), No. 3, 136–149.

CLOSS, AUGUST. "Nihilism and the Modern German Drama. Grabbe and Büchner." *Studies in German Literature.* London: Cresset Press; 1957. Pp. 147–163.

COWEN, ROY. "Identity and Conscience in Büchner's Works." *Germanic Review,* 43 (1968), 258–266.

FISCHER, HEINZ. "Some Marginal Notes on Georg Büchner." *Revue de littérature comparée,* 46 (1972), 255–258.

FLEISSNER, E. M. "Revolution as Theatre: Danton's Death and Marat/Sade," *Massachusetts Review,* 7 (1966), 543–556.

HAMBURGER, MICHAEL. "Georg Büchner." *Evergreen Review* (1957), No. i, 68–98.

HAMBURGER, MICHAEL. "Georg Büchner." In *Reason and Energy.* London: Routledge & Paul, and New York: Grove Press, 1957. Pp. 179–208.

KAUFMANN, FRIEDRICH W. "Georg Büchner." In *German Dramatists of the 19th Century.* Los Angeles: Lymanhouse, 1940. Pp. 103–111.

KAYSER, WOLFGANG. " 'Grotesk! Grotesk!'–'Woyzeck'–The Romantic Comedy." In *The Grotesque in Art and Literature,* transl. by Ulrich Weisstein. New York: McGraw-Hill, 1966. Pp. 89–99.

KNIGHT, ARTHUR H. J. "Some Considerations Relating to Georg Büch-

Selected Bibliography

ner's Opinions on History and the Drama and to his Play 'Dantons Tod.'" *Modern Language Review,* 40 (1947), 70–81.

KNIGHT, ARTHUR H. J. *Georg Büchner.* Oxford: Basil Blackwell, 1951.

KRESH, JOSEPH G. "Goerg Büchner's Reputation as an Economic Radical." *Germanic Review,* 8 (1933), 44–51.

LINDENBERGER, HERBERT S. *Georg Büchner.* Cardondale: Southern Illinois University Press, 1964.

LORAM, IAN C. "Georg Kaiser's 'Der Soldat Tanaka': Vollendeter 'Woyzeck?'" *German Life and Letters,* 10 (1956/57), 43–48.

MACLEAN, H. "The Moral Conflict in Georg Büchner's 'Dantons Tod,'" *Journal of the Australasian Modern Language Association,* 6 (May, 1957), 25–33.

MAJUT, RUDOLF. "Georg Büchner and Some English Thinkers." *Modern Language Review,* 48 (1953), 310–322.

MAJUT, RUDOLF. "Some Literary Affiliations of Georg Büchner with England." *Modern Language Review,* 50 (1955), 30–43.

MURDOCH, BRIAN. "Communication as a Dramatic Problem. Büchner, Chekhov, Hofmannsthal and Wesker." *Revue de littérature comparée,* 45 (1971), 40–56.

PARKER, JOHN J. "Some Reflections on Georg Büchner's 'Lenz' and Its Principal Sources, The Oberlin Record." *German Life and Letters,* 21 (1967/68), 103–111.

PEACOCK, RONALD. "A Note on Georg Büchner's Plays." *German Life and Letters,* 10 (1955/57), 189–197.

ROSENBERG, RALPH P. "Georg Büchner's Early Reception in America." *Journal of English and Germanic Philology,* 44 (1945), 270–273.

SCHMIDT, HENRY J. *Satire, Caricature and Perspectivism in the Works of Georg Büchner.* The Hague: Mouton, 1970.

SHAW, LEROY R. "Symbolism of Time in Georg Büchner's 'Leonce and Lena.'" *Monatshefte für deutschen Unterricht,* 48 (1956), 221–230.

STEINER, GEORGE. *The Death of Tragedy.* New York: Hill & Wang, 1963. Pp. 270–281.

STERN, JOSEPH P. "A World of Suffering: Georg Büchner." In *Re-Interpretations.* London: Thomas & Hudson, 1964. Pp. 78–155.

VICKERS, L. "Georg Büchner." *Nation,* 32 (1880), 224.

WHITE, JOHN S. "Georg Büchner or the Suffering Through the Father." *The American Imago,* 9 (1952), 365–427.

ZEIDEL, EDWIN H. "A Note on Georg Büchner and Gerhart Hauptmann," *Journal of English and Germanic Philology,* 44 (1945), 87–88.

Index

Abstraction, 137
Absurdity, 45, 82, 95, 119, 122, 129, 133, 136, 137
Abyss, 68, 71, 119, 124, 125, 135
Adelaide (Büchner character), 39, 40
Aeschylus, 14
Ala (Mrozek character), 137
Alcohol, consumption of, 84, 103, 121, 122, 126, 137
Alexander the Great, 81, 82
Alfieri, Count Vittorio, 73
Alienation, 27, 28, 67, 135
America, 19, 32, 127, 129
Andres (Büchner character), 122, 126
Animals, 118, 119, 120-21, 125, 137, 146
Arnim, Achim von, 74
Art, 56-59, 65, 120, 137
Arthur (Mrozek character), 136-37
As You Like It (Shakespeare), 73, 77, 80, 81
Atheism, 14, 45, 46, 68
Audience confrontation, 133-34
Auschwitz, 138
Autopsy of Johann Woyzeck, 101
Awakening of Spring (Wedekind), 133
Awareness, 27, 28, 38, 40, 46, 64, 78, 79, 94
Azdak (Brecht character), 135

Baal (Brecht), 129, 134
Bald Soprano, The (Ionesco), 135
Baumann, Gerhart, 140

Becker, August, 17, 18, 19, 139
Beckett, Samuel, 129, 135
Before Dawn (Hauptmann), 131
Berg, Alban, 134
Bergemann, Fritz, 134, 139
Berlin, 131
Bible, 68, 121
"Blinde, Die" (Poem by Chamisso), 86
Boredom, 70, 78, 135-36
Bourgoisie, 93, 113, 114, 145
Brain, see Nervous system
Brazil, 136
Brecht, Bertolt, 129, 134, 135, 136, 137
Brentano, Clemens, 73, 74
Brion, Friederike, 50
Büchner, Ernst (father), 13, 19
Büchner, Georg: critical reception, 19-20, 22, 24-26, 60, 72-73, 75, 76, 94, 103, 127-30, 140-41; death of, 13, 22; diary of, 22, 23, 140; esthetics of, 53-63; illness of, 17, 21-22, 50; as lecturer, 20, 21, 140; letters of, 15-16, 17, 20, 21, 22, 23, 26, 50, 54, 55, 72, 102, 106, 107; performance of plays, 75, 93, 108, 127-29; political involvement, 14-16, 17, 18, 19, 24, 30; quality of mind, 14; as scientist, 13, 14, 20, 21, 49-50, 53, 132; skepticism of, 14; as student, 14, 15, 20, 49
Büchner, Ludwig (brother), 22, 139
Büchner, Wilhelm (brother), 19, 20, 139

Büchse der Pandora, Die (Wedekind), *see Pandora's Box*
Butzbach, 18

Camille Desmoulins (Büchner character), 31, 33, 39, 44, 80
Camino Real, El (Tennessee Williams), 129
Camus, Albert, 129
Captain (Büchner character), 109, 113-17, 119, 120-21, 122, 123, 124, 133, 145, 146
Carnival, 134, 146
Cato, 14
Caucasian Chalk Circle, The (Brecht), 135
Chairs, The (Ionesco), 129
Chamisso, Adelbert von, 86
Chaos, 33, 35, 36, 47, 95, 134, 135
Chaumette (Büchner character) 45, 46
Christianity, 41, 123
Church, 110, 115, 123, 131
Clarus, Dr. Johann Christian, 94, 97-112, 122, 125, 144
Clemm, Gustav, 18, 19, 139
Clurman, Harold, 128
Commentary (magazine), 147
Comprehension, *see* Awareness
Consciousness, *see* Awareness
Cotta (publisher), 20, 72
Creation. 47, 69, 120, 121
Cynicism, 75, 83, 86, 121

Danton (Büchner character), 24-48, 68, 69, 79, 83, 84, 89, 94, 95, 102, 117, 127, 138, 141
Danton, Georges Jacques, 25-26
Danton's Death, 19, 22, 24-48, 49, 54, 55, 75, 76, 79, 80, 93, 95, 107, 112, 117, 127, 128, 129, 132, 134, 135, 138, 140-42, 143
Darmstadt, 13, 14, 15, 18, 19, 20, 21, 22
Darwin, Charles, 130
Death, 29, 48, 86-87, 116, 132, 144
Death penalty, 94, 97, 98
Decadence, 21, 30, 97, 112
Deception, *see* Illusion

Delusion, *see* Illusion
Denatured animals, 119-20
Dichter Lenz und Fridericke von Sesenheim, Der (Stöber), 49, 142
Disillusionment, 76, 78, 128
Doctor (Büchner character), 93, 101, 109, 113, 114, 116-19, 122, 123, 124, 126, 133, 136, 145, 146
Double nature, 123
Double reason, 120, 123
Drama, 26, 44, 72, 107, 109
Dramatic rhetoric, 129, 133
Dramatic structure, 26, 28, 44-45, 47, 93, 94, 95, 108, 132, 134-35, 137
Dream, 42, 43, 44, 51, 69, 75, 76, 77, 81, 83, 85, 87, 117, 123, 124, 131-32, *see also* Illusion
Drum-Major (Büchner character), 109, 121, 126
Drunkenness, *see* Intoxication
Dürrenmatt, Friedrich, 137

Earth Spirit, The (Wedekind), 133
Einem, Gottfried von, 134
Enlightenment, 34, 133
Epic Theater, 134
Epicureanism, 35, 38, 39, 40, 41
Erdgeist, Der (Wedekind), *see Earth Spirit*
Ermittlung Die (Weiss), *see Investigation*
Esthetics, 75, 107, 108, 132
Eugene (Mrozek character) 137
Execution, 24, 26, 31, 37, 42, 94, 98, 99, 104
Existentialism, 95, 130, 135
Expressionism, 28, 130, 134

Fairy tale, 74, 75, 76, 77, 89, 117
Faith, 46, 68, 70, 71, 89, 98, 101, 112, 117-18, 123
Fantasy, 76, 81, 116, 118
Faust (Goethe character), 38, 95
Faust (Goethe), 38, 39, 125
Folksong, 75
Fool, 28, 32, 73, 80, 81, 83, 85, 92, 114, 121
Form, 58, 59, 108
Foucault, Michel, 130

Index

Frankfurt, 18, 19, 138
Franz, Rudolf, 134
Franzos, Karl Emil, 23, 139, 148
Freemasonry, 98, 109
Free Stage (Freie Bühne), 131, 132
Free will, 82, 118, 146
Freud, Sigmund, 130, 132
Friederike (Büchner character), 68
Frisch, Max, 137
Frühlings Erwachen (Wedekind),
    see Awakening of Spring

Galileo (Brecht character) 135
Game of Love, The (Schnitzler),
    133
Giessen, 16, 17, 18, 19, 50
Girondins, 25-26
God, 31, 45, 46, 47, 68, 70, 89, 103,
    119, 120, 121, 123
Goddelau, 13
Goethe, Johann Wolfgang von, 14,
    33-34, 38, 49, 50, 53, 56, 90-91,
    95, 125, 142, 144
Goldwater, Senator Barry, 127
Grass, Günter, 138
Green Cockatoo, The (Schnitzler),
    132
Gretchen (Goethe character), 125
Götz von Berlichingen (Goethe), 33,
    34
Gundolf, Friedrich, 73, 74, 143
Gutzkow, Karl, 19-20, 21, 22, 72, 74,
    75

Hallucination, see Visions
Hamburger, Michael, 146
Hamlet (Shakespeare character), 29,
    77
Hamlet (Shakespeare), 80, 141
Handke, Peter, 129, 138
Hannele (Hauptmann), 131
Hauptmann, Gerhart, 131, 132
Hausenstein, Wilhelm, 134
Hebbel, Friedrich, 93, 133
Hébertists, 31
Hegelian dialectics, 14, 107
Heinrich (Goethe character in
    Werther), 90-91

Hérault de Séchelles (Büchner char-
    acter), 26, 29, 30, 31, 32, 33, 36,
    45, 46
Herder, Johann Friedrich, 50
Herr Puntila und Sein Knecht Matti
    (Brecht), 135
Hess, Johann Jakob, 140
Hesse, Grand Duchy of, 13, 14, 15,
    16, 18
Hessian Courier (Büchner-Weidig),
    18, 19, 24, 25, 30, 31
History and literature, 26, 35, 55, 62,
    95, 107, 108, 109, 111, 112, 113,
    129, 131, 137, 138, 143
Höllerer, Walter, 140
Homer, 14
Human nature, 32, 33, 34, 35, 36,
    37, 41, 67-68, 70, 71, 77, 112, 119,
    120, 130, 135
Hugo, Victor, 20
Hymnen an die Nacht (Novalis),
    144

Idealism, 54-56
Idée fixe, 44, 123, 141
Illness, 97, 100, 116
Illusion, 27, 28, 40, 42, 44, 70-71,
    77, 80, 81, 89, 100, 101, 106, 117-
    18, 123, 124, 126, 133, 138
Impressionism, 130, 132
Individualism, 32, 45
Inner voice, 86, 88, 96, 109
Insane asylum, see Madhouse
Insanity, see Madness
Instinct, 66, 86
Intellect, 27, 29, 47, 49, 79, 89, 95,
    111, 114, 118, 119, 123, 125, 126,
    130-31, 132
Intoxication, 84, 103, 104, 105, 121,
    126, 137
Investigation, The (Weiss), 138, 148
Ionesco, Eugène, 129, 136, 137, 148

Jacobins, 25, 30, 39
Jacques (Shakespeare character),
    80, 81
Jaegle, Pastor Johann Jakob, 50
Jaegle, Wilhelmine, 16, 17, 22, 23,
    50, 140

Julie (Büchner character), 26, 27, 28, 34

Kaiser, Georg, 134
Kaspar (Handke), 129
Kätchen von Heilbronn (Kleist), 74
Kaufmann (Büchner character), 54, 55
King Peter (Büchner character), 74, 82, 83, 145
Kleist, Heinrich von, 74
Knight, A.H.J., 72, 102, 108, 143, 145, 147
Knowledge, 78, 95, 118, 130, 136
König, Fritz, 140
Krapp, Helmut, 141
Kuhl, Konrad, 139

Lecroix (Büchner character), 39, 40, 144
Landau, Paul, 134
Laocoon (Lessing), 58
Law, 31, 34, 44, 94, 95, 97, 98, 102, 104, 105, 112, 144
Legal accountability, 94, 97, 98-101, 105, 112, 122
Legendre (Büchner character), 39
Lehmann, Werner R., 139, 144
Leipzig, 95, 97, 99, 103
Lena (Büchner character), 82, 86-87, 88
Leonce (Büchner character), 72-92, 95, 114, 117, 123, 135, 136
Leonce and Lena, 20, 22, 70, 72-92, 117, 129, 132, 133, 135, 143-44, 145
Lenz (Büchner character), 49-71, 79, 83, 84, 86, 89, 94, 95
Lenz, 20, 22, 49-71, 72, 75, 76, 79, 83, 107, 108, 132, 142-43
Lenz, Jacob Michael Reinhold, 49, 50, 51, 125
Lessing, Gotthold Ephraim, 58
Lesson, The (Ionesco), 136
Liebelei (Schnitzler), *see Game of Love*
Lincoln Center for the Performing Arts, 127, 128

Lindenberger, Herbert S., 72, 102, 140, 143, 145, 147
Louis Philippe, King of France, 15
Love, 29, 39, 50, 73, 76, 84, 86, 88, 116, 124, 132
Lucille (Büchner character), 80
Lucrèce Borgia (Hugo), 20
Ludwig II of Hesse, 18
Lulu (Wedekind character), 133

Madhouse, 81-83, 85, 90, 130
Madness, 44, 47, 49, 50-51, 55, 63, 65, 66, 67, 69, 70, 79, 80, 83, 85, 90-91, 94, 95-107, 130, 131, 134, 137, 142, 147, 148
Madness and Civilization (Foucault), 130
Malraux, André, 129
Man's a Man, A (Brecht), 134
Marat/de Sade (Weiss), 138
Marat, Jean Paul, 39
Maria Magdalene (Hebbel), 93
Marie (Büchner character), 93, 109, 110, 113, 121, 122, 124, 125, 126
Marie (J.M.R. Lenz character in *Die Soldaten*), 125
Marie Tudor (Hugo), 20
Marion (Büchner character), 39, 40
Martens, Wolfgang, 144, 145, 147
Marxism, 25, 32
Mayer, Hans, 102, 140, 145
Meaninglessness, 42, 46-47, 79, 114, 122
Medusa's head, 57, 58, 60, 61, 63
Melancholia, 78, 87, 114, 116
Memory, 86, 89
Mephistopheles (Goethe character), 95
Messiah, 36, 42, 43
Metamorphosis, 120
Metamorphosis of the Plant (Goethe), 142
Metternich, Klemens von, 15
Mind, *see* Intellect
Minnigerode, Karl, 18, 19
Monster, myth of, 105-106
Morality, 32, 35, 36, 41, 97, 104, 106, 112, 115, 123, 125, 133, 135

Index

Mother Courage (Brecht character), 135

Mrozek, Slawomir, 136-37, 148

Mueller, Carl R., 108, 119, 139, 143, 146

Murder, 37, 93, 94, 96, 101, 102, 103, 104, 105, 106, 108, 109, 110, 113, 122, 136, 144

Music, 134

Musset, Alfred de, 72

Myth, 77, 105, 106, 117, 118, 132

Napoleon Bonaparte, 13, 14

Narrative Perspective, 53, 72, 60-67

Narrative structure, 51-67

Nascimento, Abdias do, 136

Nation, The (magazine), 147

Naturalism, 112, 130, 131, 132, 137

Nature, 56, 79, 87, 98, 117, 118, 120-21, 122, 124, 125, 126

Necessity, 102

Nervous system, 20, 21, 28, 49, 53, 79, 116

Nestroy, Johann, 73

New York, 127

Nietzsche, Friedrich, 130

Nihilism, 29, 32, 33, 35, 38, 44, 46-47, 49-50, 69, 70-71, 76, 79, 88, 116-17, 122, 125, 131, 135, 140

Normality, 83, 95, 97, 99, 101, 106, 130

Nouvelle Héloise (Rousseau), 74

Novalis, 87, 144

Oberlin (Büchner character), 51, 52, 53, 68, 69, 83

Oberlin, Pastor Johann Friedrich, 49, 54, 107, 112, 143

Offenbach, 18, 19

"On Being Sane in Insane Places" (Rosenhan), 130

On the Cranial Nerves, 21, 49, 53

On the Nervous System of the Barbel, 20, 21, 49

Opera, 134

Ophelia (Shakespeare character), 80

Orlando (Shakespeare character), 77

Paine (Büchner character), 45, 46

Pandora's Box (Wedekind), 133

Philippeau (Büchner character), 31

Pietro Aretino, 20-21, 23

Plot, 52, 73, 75, 93

Poetry and Truth (Goethe), 50, 142

Politics, 15-16, 30, 31, 32, 35, 36, 37, 41, 82, 89, 112-13, 123, 127, 128

Positivism, 116, 117

Poverty, 35, 45, 95, 102, 103, 112, 113, 124-25, 131

Prayer, 66, 68, 96, 104, 135

President of the Council of State (Büchner character), 82

Press, 95, 98, 127, 138

Professor (Ionesco character), 136

Proletarian tragedy, 93

Psychology, 53, 65, 68, 78, 85, 94, 97, 107, 108, 111, 112, 114, 117, 130, 147, 148

Rationality-Irrationality, 34, 45, 81, 94, 95

Realism, 132

Reality, 28, 29, 42, 44, 46, 54, 55, 56, 61, 64, 65, 68-69, 70, 71, 75, 77, 88, 90, 95, 106, 116, 117, 131-32, 133, 138

Reason, 81, 94, 95, 120

Reign of Terror, 24, 26, 33, 36, 43

Religion, 68, 69, 89, 97, 98, 101, 112, 117, 123, 131

Richardson, Jack, 129, 138

Robespierre (Büchner character), 25, 30, 31, 32, 33, 34, 35, 36, 37, 40, 41, 42, 43, 44, 117, 127

Robespierre, Maximilien de, 43

Romantic comedy, 74-75

Romanticism, 75, 76, 77, 87, 95, 123, 124

Romeo (Shakespeare character), 77

Ronde, La (Schnitzler), 132

Rosalie (Büchner character), 39-40

Rosenhan, D. L., 130, 147

Rousseau, Jean Jacques, 31, 74

Saint-Just (Büchner character), 25, 30, 31, 42, 117

Sanity, 44, 71, 94, 125, 130, 131, 147

Sartre, Jean Paul, 129
Sauerländer, J. D., 19-20
Schiller, Friedrich, 55, 128
Schizophrenia, 49, 51
Schnitzler, Artur, 132, 133
Schoolmaster (Büchner character), 82
Schulz, Caroline, 21-22, 23, 140
Schulz, Wilhelm Friedrich, 21-22
Science, 116, 118, 130, 136
Science (magazine), 147
Scientific instinct, 119, 122
Scientific method, 108, 112, 119, 130-31
"Sehnsucht nach dem Tode" (Novalis), see Yearning for Death
Senses, The, 28, 34, 38, 57, 69
Sexuality, 29, 30, 84, 95, 96, 104, 115-16, 131-32, 137
Shakespeare, William, 14, 29, 56, 72, 73, 80, 81
Silone, Ignazio, 129
Skepticism, 38, 46, 79, 100-101, 114, 116
Société des Droits l'Homme et du Citoyen, 15, 18
Society for Human Rights, 18, 24
Soldaten, Die (Lenz), 125
Sophocles, 14
Sorrows of Young Werther, The (Goethe), 90-91, 142, 144
Sternheim, Carl, 134
Stöber, August, 49, 142
Stomil (Mrozek character), 137
Storm and Stress, 33, 34, 41, 49, 50, 125
Strasbourg, 14, 15, 16, 17, 20, 21, 49, 50
Structuralism, 130
Suicide, 14, 19, 38, 70, 88, 96, 144
Sunken Bell, The (Hauptmann), 132
Sur le système nerveux du barbeau, see On the Nervous System of the Barbel

Tango (Mrozek), 136-37, 148
Tennessee Williams, 129
Terror, 36, 42, 67

Thinking, Process of, 28, 83, 103, 114, 115, 122
Theater of the Absurd, 129, 135-36
Time, 40, 52, 110, 113-14, 115, 141
Time (magazine), 127, 138, 147
Tieck, Ludwig, 73, 142
Toller, Ernst, 134
Touchstone (Shakespeare character), 81
Tragedy, human, 38, 44, 47, 79, 95, 106-107, 112, 122, 123, 125, 132, 133, 136, 137
Trotzki in Exile (Weiss), 138

Unideal nature, 121, 125, 126, 133

Valerio (Büchner character), 80, 81, 82, 83, 84, 85, 86, 88, 89, 114, 117
Viëtor, Karl, 72, 76, 102, 139, 140, 141, 143, 145
Visions (hallucinations), 99, 100, 102, 103, 110, 111, 117-18, 131
Vivian Beaumont Theater (New York), 127, 128
Volksmärchen, 75
Vor Sonnenaufgang (Hauptmann), see Before Dawn

Waiting for Godot (Beckett), 129, 135
Waldbach in Steinthal, 49, 64
Wallenstein's Death (Schiller), 128
Weavers, The (Hauptmann), 131
Wedekind, Frank, 133, 134
Weidig, Friedrich Ludwig, 18, 19, 139
Weiss, Peter, 138, 148
Werther (Goethe character), 90-91
Werther (Goethe), see Sorrows of Young Werther
Wienbarg, Ms., 110
Wiese, Benno von, 140
Witkowski, Georg, 134
Women, 27, 84, 125, 133
Woost, Mrs., 95, 96, 109, 110
Woyzeck (Büchner character), 93-126

Index

Woyzeck, 20-21, 23, 75, 76, 93-126, 128, 129, 132, 133, 134, 135, 137, 143, 144-47
Woyzeck, Johann, 93, 95-107, 108-11, 122, 130
Wozzeck, 134, 148

Yearning for death, 29, 86-87
Yearning for Death (Novalis), 144

Young Worker (Büchner character), 121, 126, 147
Yountville, Calif., 129

Zeitschrift für Staatsarzneikunde, 145
Zurich, 13, 21, 22, 140
Züricher Zeitung, 22
Zweig, Arnold, 134

DATE DUE

GAYLORD			PRINTED IN U.S.A.